# Service Science

Concepts, Technology, Management

*Harry Katzan, Jr.*

**iUniverse, Inc.**
**New York  Bloomington**

# Service Science

## Concepts, Technology, Management

Copyright © 2008 by Harry Katzan, Jr.

iUniverse books may be ordered through booksellers or by contacting:

iUniverse
1663 Liberty Drive
Bloomington, IN 47403
www.iuniverse.com
1-800-Authors (1-800-288-4677)

ISBN: 978-0-595-52519-5 (pbk)
ISBN: 978-0-595-51264-5 (cloth)
ISBN: 978-0-595-62572-7 (ebk)

Printed in the United States of America

iUniverse rev. date: 11/03/08

To Margaret, as always

# *Forward*

In today's fast paced world of globalization, advanced technology, and customer expectations, nearly everyone wants to keep up with the latest information that affects their job and personal life, as well as business and government strategy. Customer focused organizations are the key to competitive advantage and an evolving body of knowledge called *service science* helps everyone understand how to design and operate such an organization.

*Service science* is defined as the application of scientific, engineering, and management competencies that a service-provider organization performs that creates value for the benefit of the client or customer. Often the "service" is co-produced on demand. Many academics and practicing managers have helped build this body of knowledge since the 1980s in disciplines such as service marketing, human resource management, and service operations. Recently, IBM has promoted service science as a new framework to integrate a wide variety of disciplines whereby an organization can gain a competitive advantage and build long-term customer relationships.

Harry Katzan's new book, titled *Service Science: Concepts, Technology, Management,* continues to build upon previous work. It is an honor and a pleasure to recommend this book as a thought leader on the topic of service science. My favorite saying by an unknown author is "Do not follow where the path may lead. Go instead where there is no path and leave a trail." Each author, researcher, and practicing manager makes contributions to this evolving field of study and this book leads us down new paths of thought and understanding.

Dr. David A. Collier
Eminent Scholar, Alico Chair in Operations Management
Lutgert College of Business
Florida Gulf Coast University
Fort Myers, Florida
June, 2008

# *Introduction*

Recognizing that more than 80% of the country's GNP results from services and also that more than 80% of the workforce is employed in services, Sam Palmisano, CEO of IBM, initiated a corporate-wide program in Service Science that has transformed IBM and many other organizations. The cornerstone of the program is the fact that even though most of us are engaged in services, we really know very little about the subject. At the time, there was no academic subject called "service science," no principles of service science, no theorems, and most importantly, there was no set of best practices. He has changed all of that. An important aspect of the IBM initiative is that it has enabled academic participation in the development of the subject matter through the establishment of a field called **Service Science** in a similar manner to the way IBM assisted in the development of academic programs in Computer Science, three decades ago.

To set the stage for further discussion, Service Science relates to traditional services (such as medical provisioning, banking, insurance, and a variety of personal services), Internet and informational services, business organization and operations, consulting, government, education, software development, and even sports and recreation – to name only a few areas. One person has described the operation of the human body as a collection of services and another has developed a DNA of services.

Service Science is an interesting subject in its own right. The New York Times author and writer Thomas Friedman set the stage for the subject matter as it relates to globalization in the winter of 2006 in his book entitled *The World is Flat*. Clearly, globalization is a key area of engagement, with regard to Service Science, and there appears to be a large amount of international interest in the subject matter.

We are additionally listing several interesting components of Service Science, to promote further discussion:

Service concepts
Service modeling
Service systems
Information services
Service management
Service technology
Service architecture

There is a high level of interest in Service Science since it has the potential to change the way we think about and subsequently view the new world order. Will Service Science eventually change the predominant economic focus from products to services?

The preface is followed by a listing of the 2007 U.S. National Investment Act, which may give some evidence to the direction things are heading.

Responding to this situation, the IBM Corporation initiated a project in the years 2005-2006 to develop a science of services. The project has resulted in tidal wave of activity within businesses and universities to study the subject and develop academic programs. The generic title for programs of this type is Service Science, Management, and Engineering (SSME) with Service Science as its basis. Corresponding academic programs are already in place in many universities in the US, England, and Germany.

Since service is the cornerstone of most modern businesses, there is a high level of interest in the subject by persons from business, government, and education. The IBM Corporation has supported intellectual activity on the subject by giving introductory presentations at many conferences and by providing liberal access to relevant information on corporate Web sites. The subject of service science has been addressed in papers in most business and computer conferences, usually in the area of service management and service marketing because a clear description of exactly what constitutes service science has not heretofore been available.

This is the first book on Service Science and its main objective is to introduce this new and exciting field.

# Preface

Service Science is an exciting new field for academicians and practitioners, because it is the up and coming discipline for the 21$^{st}$ century. Services are important to people in business, government, education, health care and management, religion, military, scientific research, engineering, and other endeavors that are too numerous to mention. The subject is of interest to providers and consumers of services, alike. In fact, most service providers – be they individuals, businesses, governments, and so forth – are also consumers of services.

Today, most of us are employed in services. Typical examples are doctors, dentists, lawyers, teachers, entertainers, news people, dry cleaners, and maintenance workers. Actually, this should not be a surprise, since much of what we do in everyday life involves using services. Service activity is characterized by the fact that the results are usually intangible, meaning in this case that an artifact of some sort is not produced as a result of a service experience, as it is in the manufacture of products. It would seem as though some definitions are in order to get the ball rolling.

A *service* is a client/provider interaction that creates and captures value, and a *service system* is a system of people and technology that adapts to the changing value of knowledge in the system. *Service science* is the study of service systems.

To be more specific, a *service system* is a socially constructed collection of service events in which participants exchange beneficial actions through a knowledge-based strategy that captures value from a provider-client relationship. The inherent service strategy is a dynamic process that orchestrates or coordinates components, employees, partners, and clients in the co-production of value. Based on a theoretical framework for creating economies of coordination, research on service science incorporates a microanalysis of various and diverse service events, so as to develop a view of the services landscape.

*Service Science* is an abstraction of service systems in the same way that computer science is an abstraction of computer-based information systems. The procedure, in both cases, is to take a piece of an existing system and put it under the microscope of academic scrutiny. In this particular instance, we are taking a service centric view of enterprise systems, where traditional enterprise functions are candidates for being packaged as enterprise services.

This book is an introduction to Service Science for people in business, education, and government. It can be used as a textbook and a professional book. Each of the eight chapters ends with a comprehensive summary, a list of key words, a few good questions, and a set of selected readings. In fact, the book ends with a list of reference books to assist in developing a service library. They are all recommended, but as things are in everyday life, some would be more recommended than others based on individual preferences.

Chapter one, entitled *Understanding Services*, is the key chapter. It is easy to read and totally accessible to all readers. It sets the framework for the rest of the book and would be useful for persons from all walks of life. Essentially, this chapter covers what services are.

Chapter two, entitled *Service Models*, gives the five dimensions along which we can classify services:

I.   *Service Process* – using the degrees of Customer Interaction and Customization (by the provider) and Provider Judgment or Labor Intensity as metrics

II.  *Service Nature* – using the Service Object and Service Result as metrics

III. *Service Delivery* – using Service Scheduling  and Service Mode (continuous or discrete) as metrics

IV.  *Service Availability* – using Service Site and Service Execution (who travels – provider or client) as metrics

V.   *Service Demand* – using Demand Fluctuation and Service Capacity as metrics

We can use the five dimensions as service model generators. A DNA of services is developed; it goes a long way towards explaining why doctors and dentists are in one category, and Internet service and homeowner services are in other categories.

Chapter three, entitled *Service Systems*, describes services as a collection of resources and economic entities, capable of engaging in or supporting one or more service events. The resources are the infrastructure and other facilities necessary to support the service process. The economic entities are the service provider and service client that co-produce the service event. In the case of possession processing services, the service environment consists of one or more tangible objects that serve as the service object of a service process. In this sense, the service object is referred to as the *"operand* of the service process." In most cases, a service system is required to sustain a service event.

Chapter four, entitled *Information Services*, describes how information and communications technology (ICT) has enhanced how we live and work. An *information service* is a resource capable of supporting a service event or instantiating a service event based on information. In other words, an information service can assist in the execution of a service, such as in retailing, or it can actually be the service as when buying a pair of shoes on the Internet or looking up something on the World Wide Web. The resource is a service provider that can take the form of a person or a computer. The execution of an information service event requires a service client that can also take the form of a person or computer and the provider and client must interact in order to co-produce the service.

Chapter five, entitled *Service management*, moves the subject of services into the realm of management. Through the application of information and communications technology (ICT), many organizations have encapsulated everyday operations enabling them to go through a transformational process to achieve revenue growth by being able to respond more quickly to changing market conditions and by being more effective and efficient in the application of services. This chapter describes modern services management.

Chapter six, entitled *Services Technology*, describes how service providers and client use communications and computer technology to sustain service events. This chapter covers the constituent technology, such as web services, XML, protocols, and relevant methods. This is the most complicated chapter in the book and can serve as a doorway to some of the latest concepts in Internet technology.

Chapter seven, entitled *Service Architecture*, covers how to design systems and construct computer applications from components and services. Service-oriented architecture is covered as a set of architectural design principles, rather than as a product. The emphasis in this chapter is on aligning solutions with business processes and the creation of agile business performance.

Chapter eight, entitled *Service Business*, completes the structure of the discipline of Service Science. This is an eclectic chapter that relates Service Science to the worlds of business, education, and government.

Welcome to our new world.

Thanks to Margaret Katzan for helping with the project.

Harry Katzan, Jr.
*Hilton Head, South Carolina*

# The U.S. National Innovation Investment Act

US House and Senate voted to approve on August 2nd, 2007; President has signed.

## SEC. 1106. STUDY OF SERVICE SCIENCE.

(a) Sense of Congress- It is the sense of Congress that, in order to strengthen the competitiveness of United States enterprises and institutions and to prepare the people of the United States for high-wage, high-skill employment, the Federal Government should better understand and respond strategically to the emerging management and learning discipline known as service science.

(b) Study- Not later than 270 days after the date of enactment of this Act, the Director of the Office of Science and Technology Policy, through the National Academy of Sciences, shall conduct a study and report to Congress regarding how the Federal Government should support, through research, education, and training, the emerging management and learning discipline known as service science.

(c) Outside Resources- In conducting the study under subsection (b), the National Academy of Sciences shall consult with leaders from 2- and 4-year institutions of higher education, as defined in section 101(a) of the Higher Education Act of 1965 (20 U.S.C. 1001(a)), leaders from corporations, and other relevant parties.

(d) Service Science Defined- In this section, the term 'service science' means curricula, training, and research programs that are designed to teach individuals to apply scientific, engineering, and management disciplines that integrate elements of computer science, operations research, industrial engineering, business strategy, management sciences, and social and legal sciences, in order to encourage innovation in how organizations create value for customers and shareholders that could not be achieved through such disciplines working in isolation.

# Contents

**Forward**............................................................................**vii**

**Introduction**.......................................................................**ix**

**Preface** ................................................................................**xi**

**1    UNDERSTANDING SERVICES** ........................................**1**

Employment And The Service Sector .......................................1
Service – A Personal Dimension .............................................2
Service – A Professional Dimension.........................................2
Business Services ....................................................................4
Differences Between Products And Services..............................4
Classification Of Services .......................................................5
    *Service Criteria*................................................................6
    *People Processing Services*..................................................6
    *Possession Processing Services*.............................................6
    *Information Processing Services*..........................................7
Characteristics Of Services .....................................................7
Summary.................................................................................9
Key Terminology ..................................................................10

Selected Reading ................................................................. 11

**2    SERVICE MODELS** ...................................... **13**

Social Constructionism ...................................................... 13
Concepts, Classes, And Service Events................................ 14
*The Notion of a Service Model* ..................................... *14*
*Concepts*........................................................................ *15*
*Service Classes and Events* ............................................ *15*
*Multiplicity of Service Classes in a Service Universe* ............... *16*
*Service Models and Specificity*........................................ *16*
*Service Attributes*.......................................................... *17*
*Service Dimensions* ...................................................... *17*
*Service Process* ............................................................. *18*
*Service Nature*.............................................................. *19*
*Service Delivery*............................................................ *20*
*Service Availability*........................................................ *20*
*Service Demand* ........................................................... *21*
*Epilogue to the Service Dimensions* ............................... *22*
The DNA Of Services ........................................................ 23
*Characterization of the Service Matrices*........................ *23*
*Quadrant-Based Scale*.................................................. *24*
*Additional Examples of Service DNA Sequences* .............. *25*
*Client Travels* ............................................................... *27*
*Client Travels* ............................................................... *27*
*Provider Travels* ........................................................... *27*
*Provider Travels* ........................................................... *27*
*No Travel* ..................................................................... *27*
*No Travel* ..................................................................... *27*
*Information Systems Service DNA Sequence* ................... *28*
Models, Classes, And Objects............................................ 28
Summary........................................................................... 29
Key Terminology .............................................................. 29
Selected Reading .............................................................. 31

**3    SERVICE SYSTEMS** ................................... **33**

Systems Concepts.............................................................. 33
*Relationships* ............................................................... *34*

Environment ..............................................................34
System Attributes .....................................................34
Service Systems Ontology ........................................35
Reductionist View .....................................................35
Service Provisioning ......................................................36
The Service Facility....................................................36
The Service Shop .......................................................37
The Service Portal......................................................37
Mobile Service Facilities ..........................................38
Client Facilities ..........................................................38
Service Implementation ...............................................38
Generic Functions Performed During Service .......39
Generic Operations Performed to Achieve Service ...40
Business Service Systems ..............................................41
Globalization .............................................................41
Information and Communications Technology.......42
Business Agility ..........................................................42
Outsourcing................................................................42
Offshoring ..................................................................43
Outsourcing and Offshoring ....................................44
Transformational Outsourcing..................................44
Sharing........................................................................44
Composite Services ....................................................45
Service Process Organization ......................................45
Expectations ...............................................................46
An Organization Example – Retailing and Services ...46
Service, Service Providers, and Service Process.......46
Up a Notch .................................................................47
Transitional Service Organization Model ...............47
Summary..........................................................................48
Key Terminology ............................................................48
Selected Reading ............................................................50

**4    INFORMATION SERVICES.........................................51**

Information Service Concepts .......................................51
A Personal Dimension...............................................52
Data versus Information.............................................52

*Ordinary Mail* ............................................................. *53*
*Is Software a Service?* ...................................................... *53*
Enterprise Information Services ........................................ *54*
*"About" Information* ...................................................... *54*
*Business Information* ...................................................... *55*
*Transaction Services* ...................................................... *55*
*Information Processing* .................................................... *56*
*Client and Provider Input to an Information Service* .......... *57*
*Interaction Services* ....................................................... *57*
*Service Bus* ................................................................... *58*
*Collaboration* ............................................................... *59*
Information Service Applications ..................................... *59*
*Pull versus Push* ............................................................ *60*
*Enterprise Service Constituents* ........................................ *61*
*Information Service Model* ............................................... *61*
*Scope of Electronic Information Services* .............................. *62*
*Electronic Commerce* ...................................................... *63*
*Electronic Business* ........................................................ *64*
*Electronic Marketplace* ................................................... *66*
*Electronic Government* .................................................... *66*
Personal Information Services .......................................... *67*
*Chat Rooms* .................................................................. *68*
*Instant Messaging* .......................................................... *68*
*Front and Back Stages* .................................................... *69*
*Internet Telephone* ......................................................... *69*
*Web Auctions* ................................................................ *70*
*User Generated Media* ..................................................... *70*
*Social Networking* .......................................................... *71*
*Newsgroups* ................................................................... *72*
Summary ..................................................................... *72*
Key Terminology .......................................................... *73*
Selected Reading .......................................................... *75*

**5    SERVICE MANAGEMENT ............................................ 77**

Service Management Concepts ......................................... 78
*Information Technology* ................................................... *78*
*Domain of Service Management* ......................................... *79*

Service as a Business.............................................................80
Service Componentization.....................................................81
Service Management Lifecycle....................................................82
IT Services Sourcing..............................................................82
IT Services Management........................................................83
Elements of the Service Lifecycle............................................84
Service Strategy.....................................................................84
Service Design ......................................................................86
Service Transition .................................................................86
Service Operation .................................................................87
Continuous Improvement......................................................87
Postscript to the Service Management Lifecycle.......................87
Service Constraint Management.................................................88
Constraint Management Concepts...........................................88
Constraint Management Process..............................................88
Bottlenecks ...........................................................................89
Virtual Workforce .................................................................89
Drum, Buffer, Rope .............................................................90
Thinking Processes ...............................................................90
Value Nets.............................................................................90
Goods Models and Service Paradigms .....................................91
The Pull Model for Service Agility ........................................91
Service Quality..........................................................................92
Service Quality Concepts........................................................93
Client's View of Service Quality .............................................93
Client Education ...................................................................93
Client Interaction .................................................................94
Process View of Service Quality..............................................94
Enterprise View of Quality ....................................................95
E-Services...................................................................................95
E-Services Concepts................................................................96
E-Service Characteristics ........................................................96
Utility Computing Services....................................................96
E-Service Architecture ...........................................................97
Summary....................................................................................97
Key Terminology .......................................................................99
Selected Reading .....................................................................100

**6  SERVICE TECHNOLOGY........................ 103**

Service Technology Concepts .................................. 103
  *Messaging Basics* ............................................ *104*
  *Conceptual Model of Service Orientation* ........................ *105*
  *Enterprise Service Technology* ................................. *105*
  *Service Science Abstraction* .................................. *106*
Service Messaging .............................................. 106
  *Message Characterization* .................................... *107*
  *Message Patterns* ........................................... *107*
  *Message Structure* ........................................... *107*
  *Message Topology* ............................................ *108*
  *Message Interactions* ......................................... *109*
Services On The Internet And The World Wide Web ............. 110
  *Simple Mail Model* ........................................... *111*
  *Web Services Model* .......................................... *113*
  *HyperText Transfer Protocol* .................................. *115*
HyperText Markup Language .................................... 116
  *HTML Documents* ............................................ *117*
  *Tags* ..................................................... *118*
  *Discovery* .................................................. *118*
  *Document Elements* .......................................... *119*
  *Dynamic Linking* ............................................ *120*
Extensible Markup Language ................................... 122
  *Rendering an XML Document* .................................. *123*
  *XML Attributes* ............................................. *125*
  *Document Type Declaration* .................................. *125*
  *Character Data* ............................................. *127*
  *DTD Attributes* ............................................. *129*
  *XML Schema* ................................................ *130*
  *Additional XML Features* ..................................... *132*
Web Services .................................................. 133
  *Web Service Concepts* ........................................ *133*
  *Web Service Model* .......................................... *135*
  *Web Services Description Language Operations* ................. *137*
  *Universal Description, Discovery, and Integration Operations* .... *138*
  *Web Service Goal* ........................................... *139*
Summary ...................................................... 139

Key Terminology ................................................................. 141
A Few Good Questions ..................................................... 142
Selected Reading ............................................................... 143

**7   SERVICE ARCHITECTURE ............................................. 145**

Service Architecture Concepts ......................................... 145
   *Solution Life Cycle* ...................................................... *147*
   *On Demand* ................................................................. *147*
   *Components, Services, and Functions* ......................... *148*
   *Service Orientation* ...................................................... *149*
Service-Oriented Architecture Overview ......................... 149
   *Incremental Development* ............................................ *150*
   *Business Models* .......................................................... *150*
   *Componentization* ........................................................ *152*
   *Specialization* ............................................................... *153*
   *Locality and Interoperability* ...................................... *153*
Service-Oriented Business Infrastructure ........................ 153
   *Business Component Viewpoint* ................................... *153*
   *Technology-Centric Viewpoint* ..................................... *155*
Service Development ......................................................... 155
   *Phased Approach to Service Development* ................... *155*
   *Legacy Systems* ............................................................ *156*
   *Exposing Functionality in Legacy Systems* .................. *157*
Service Reference Architecture ........................................ 158
   *Loose Coupling* ............................................................ *158*
   *Services* ......................................................................... *159*
   *Messaging* ..................................................................... *159*
   *Registry* ......................................................................... *160*
   *Architecture Services Management* ............................. *160*
   *Orchestration* ............................................................... *161*
   *Analysis* ......................................................................... *162*
   *User Interaction* ........................................................... *162*
Service Architecture Principles ........................................ 162
   *Service Abstraction* ...................................................... *163*
   *Service Encapsulation* .................................................. *163*
   *Service Loose Coupling* ................................................ *163*
   *Service Contract* ........................................................... *164*

Service Reusability .................................................... 164
Service Composability ................................................ 164
Service Autonomy .................................................... 164
Service Discoverability................................................ 165
Service Architecture Structure And Operation ...................... 165
Enterprise Systems.................................................... 165
Service Architecture Structure ..................................... 165
Enterprise Service Bus .............................................. 166
Service Manager ..................................................... 167
Service Architecture Operation..................................... 167
Summary................................................................ 167
Key Terminology ..................................................... 170
A Few Good Questions .............................................. 171
Selected Reading ..................................................... 172

**8    SERVICE BUSINESS ....................................... 173**

Service Business Concepts ........................................... 173
Business Model ...................................................... 174
Strategy and Mission................................................. 174
Service Ecosystem Characteristics.................................. 174
Strategic Assets ...................................................... 175
Service Context....................................................... 175
Service Perspective................................................... 176
Service Systems Thinking ........................................... 176
Service Factors ...................................................... 177
Service Creationism ................................................. 177
Service Evolutionism ................................................ 178
Service Underpinnings .............................................. 179
Value Creation ...................................................... 180
Availability, Capacity, Continuity, Security, and Risk .......... 180
Service Assets ....................................................... 181
Service Portfolio..................................................... 181
Operations Framework................................................ 181
Service-Level Management ........................................... 184
Availability Management ........................................... 184
Capacity Management ............................................... 185
Service-Desk Management............................................ 185

Incident Management.................................................185
Problem Management..............................................185
Change Management...............................................185
Relationship of Key Processes...............................186
Directory-Services Management..........................186
Governance..................................................................186
Corporate Governance............................................186
Information Technology Governance ...................187
Service Governance..................................................187
Summary......................................................................187
Key Terminology.......................................................188
A Few Good Questions ...........................................189
Selected Reading .......................................................190
**Recommended Reading** ..............................................**193**
**Index** ..........................................................................**197**

# 1

# Understanding Services

The subject of services is in the news, because it is the up and coming discipline for the 21$^{st}$ century. It is more significant than technology, entrepreneurship, business growth, and innovation. In fact, services encompass all of the subjects mentioned. Services are important to people in business, government, education, health care and management, religion, military, scientific research, engineering, and other endeavors that are too numerous to mention. The subject is of interest to providers and consumers of services, alike. In fact, most service providers – be they individuals, businesses, governments, and so forth – are also consumers of services.

## EMPLOYMENT AND THE SERVICE SECTOR

Today, most of us are employed in services. Typical examples are doctors, dentists, lawyers, teachers, entertainers, news people, dry cleaners, and maintenance workers. Actually, this should not be a surprise, since much of what we do in everyday life involves using services.

Service activity is characterized by the fact that the results are usually intangible, meaning in this case that an artifact of some sort is not produced as a result of a service experience, as it is in the manufacture of products.

# SERVICE – A PERSONAL DIMENSION

Most of us want to do better – in our jobs, education, business, professions, and so forth, and when we purchase services, it is really important that we get the best service for our time and money. But without a clear understanding of exactly what it is that constitutes a service, what differentiates one service from another, and how services operate and interoperate, continuous improvement will be a never-ending process of trial and error.

The concept of service has its roots in economic activities that are classified as extractive, secondary, and services. *Extractive* refers to agriculture, mining, forestry, fishing, and so forth. *Secondary* refers to manufacturing and processing. *Services* refer to everything else, usually subdivided into domestic, trade and commerce, information services, and personal. This is a very general definition intended for the reporting by the government of economic conditions. In order to get a handle on services, we need better definitions.

A *service* is a provider/client interaction that creates and captures value. A unique characteristic of services, unlike agriculture and manufacturing, is that both parties participate in the transaction, and in the process, both capture value. In a sense, the provider and the client co-produce the service event, because one can't do without the other. It stands to reason that the roles of the client and the provider are different. In a doctor/patient service event, for example, the physician brings knowledge, time, and the necessary infrastructure. The patient brings him or herself, a medical history, and a perceived situation that requires attention. During the service process, the participants exchange information in various forms, resulting in a change to the people involved. The doctor's experience level and assets change, as do the patient's information level and physical or mental condition. There is more to it, of course, but this is the basic idea.

# SERVICE – A PROFESSIONAL DIMENSION

In business, the case is slightly different. Some companies, such as professional firms, are totally service oriented. Other service companies, such as airlines and restaurants, have more complicated arrangements. An airline company, for example, could contract out its telephone service to another company, perhaps in another country, called *outsourcing*. In this scenario, agreements, specifying responsibilities and expectations, are required, in most cases, to enhance the benefits to both parties.

In government, services are governed by convention and law. Constituents use governmental resources for information and a variety of physical services.

In many cases, it is difficult to tell who is providing the service and who is receiving it.

In education, the provider/client relationship can be complex. Who is the provider and who is the client? Let's assume that the teacher provides the service to the student, by giving lectures and managing classroom activity. But it could be more complicated than that. Consider a university setting. Does the professor provide a service to the administration by teaching courses and doing the myriad of other things faculty do? But then again, one could look at it the other way around by contending that the purpose of the administration is to provide the educational infrastructure. So the teacher could be a provider of services and a client of services, at the same time. We will take a look at complex service arrangements in follow-on sections of this chapter and in later chapters..

Returning to the airline example, let's assume that an agreement is made with a company in another country to run a call center whereby passengers can make reservations and obtain information. Ostensibly, the objective is to save money, improve the bottom line, and help the top management look good to the shareholders. The airline is the client and the call center company is the provider. How does the client (that is the airline company, in this case), who is a stakeholder with something to gain or lose, effectively control the situation? They collectively draw up a *service level agreement* that governs the quality of service, the number of calls to be handled in a specified period of time, the duration of the agreement, and the costs involved. Why don't the patient and the doctor have a service level agreement? They do, but it is implicit in the social setting in which medical services are performed.

There is another twist to the airline example. Where do you and I – the passengers – fit in? Again, the call center operator provides an airline related service to us and we are the clients, even though we are, in fact, the provider of the financial resources that make the whole process work. The call center company effectively has two clients: the airline at the macro level and the set of passengers at the micro level.

It is commonplace for services to exist at two or more levels, as demonstrated by the airline example, in a service arrangement called a *service package*. In a service package, services are performed at differing levels and the service level agreement must reflect that eventuality. When a collection of service processes exist and they are all performed at the same level, it is called a *service bundle*. So if you go to a medical facility comprised of a team of doctors that essentially perform the same kinds of things, the set of service events is a service bundle. It follows in the case of the airline, that the service package contains a service bundle consisting of a group of telephone operators that provide services to passengers.

## BUSINESS SERVICES

Some firms further complicate the picture by essentially being in two related service businesses at the same time. Consider an information technology (IT) company that provides services in two forms: consulting and outsourcing. With consulting, the firm tells a client how to do something, and with outsourcing, the firm does it for the client. As an example, the IT firm could advise on what information systems the client needs and then develop those systems. Similarly, it could provide information on how to set up an IT operation and then run that shop after it is set up.

Related to IT services is a general class of activities known as *business services*. With business services, like IT services, there are two options: consulting and outsourcing.[1] With business service consulting, organizations are advised about business function, such as customer relationship management (CRM) and enterprise resource planning (ERP). Then, with outsourcing, the business services firm does it for you – perhaps in the areas of finance and accounting.

What we have at this point are multiple organizations, collections of people and technology connected by value propositions[2] and shared information, operating as a service system. More specifically, a *service system* is defined as a configuration of people and technology connected to another system of people and technology in order to co-create value for both organizations.

## DIFFERENCES BETWEEN PRODUCTS AND SERVICES

It is useful to consider the differences between products and services. Products are tangible and services are intangible. Now that is a pretty general statement. An automobile, a garment, a table, and even a fast-food hamburger are examples of products. A doctor's visit, swimming pool cleaning, and package delivery are examples of services. On the surface, one could conclude that products are produced through some relevant sequence of operations, but that is not a defining characteristic, since most services also go through a sequence of steps. The answer is that a product is an artifact – something you can see or touch. Clearly, a service results in something worthwhile – otherwise, why engage in it – but the result is a change in a person or possession, not in the creation of something.

---

[1] A good description of the conundrum of business service is given in Maglio and Zysman (2007).

[2] A *value proposition* is a meaningful statement of what an organization, customer, or person expects to receive from using a service.

Products are storable; services are non-storable. You can store any of the examples of products, given above. If you have your car cleaned or your lawn mowed, you can't exactly save that service. When a service is finished, it is done forever. Perhaps, a record of the service is archived, explicitly or implicitly, but once the stop button is pushed, that service machine is off. If a service has to be repeated, then it is another service event.

Another related difference is that services are generally regarded as perishable. The implication here is that if a seat on an airline flight is not used, then the value of that opportunity is lost. There are many parallels between services and events in everyday life. If you buy a fresh banana and don't eat it within a reasonable time period, its value is lost. You can buy another, but again, that is a different thing.

With products, consumption follows production. In fact, the build-store-sell and the sell-build-ship business models apply here. With services, consumption and production occur at the same time. This characteristic is related to the difference between product quality and service quality. With products, a quality assessment can be made before the customer enters the scene. With services, the client's view of quality is determined during the service process.

As product classes mature, they become standardized and competition shifts to price. Services are almost always customized. In general, product development is capital intensive, and the delivery of services is labor intensive.

It is important to recognize, however, that the creation of products may include services in the production process, and that services may also accompany production in the form of follow-on activity.

## CLASSIFICATION OF SERVICES

Given that services are pervasive in modern economies, there would appear to be so much diversity between them that it would be impossible to make any sense of the subject. After all, there does not seem to be much similarity between a lawn mowing operation and a service package for an airline – as simple examples. On the other hand, there has to be a set of common denominators that we could use to classify services so that we could draw some conclusions about organization, performance, and quality. After all, most of us would agree that clients would like to get the most for their money and providers would like to receive the greatest return on their investment of knowledge, time, and effort.

## Service Criteria

Services are generally classified by at least five criteria, although one criterion dominates. The minor factors are degree of provider labor intensity, degree of customer interaction, level of provider knowledge, and the amount of client information, that are quantitative measures brought to a service event. The major factor is a qualitative attribute known as "service nature," consisting of a service object and a service result. We will also identify other factors in the second chapter and refine the material given here when we establish a set of comprehensive service models. We will focus on the service object in this chapter, because it reflects whether a service is performed on a person, a possession, or information. In a previous section, we covered the subject of distinguishing services from goods. The service object is useful for distinguishing services from services, and it preserves the roles of the provider and the client. In a generic sense, the provider does the work and the client pays for it, and the question of who or what gets the service is the determining factor in exactly how much of the other four quantitative criteria are applied to a particular service event.

## People Processing Services

In people processing services, the provider performs corporeal actions to the client. The client is part of the service production process and remains in the domain of the provider during service delivery. There is simultaneity of production with consumption in a people processing service event, and the provider and client, are regarded as co-producing the service. A trip to the dentist typifies this type of service, as does a reservation made through an airline call center. A people processing service can change either the physical state of a person, the mental state of a person, or both. The physical state is something like increased fitness, manicured finger nails, or the location of a person. The mental state deals with non-physical attributes, such as increased knowledge, mental capability, or mental agility. Many people processing services do both, as in medical services and sports coaching.

## Possession Processing Services

In possession processing services, the provider changes the state of one or more tangible objects under the jurisdiction of the client. Many possession processing services are straightforward, as in car washing and other maintenance activities. These services relate to the condition of an object and are regarded as physical services. Clearly, there are other attributes of service objects and one of the most common is ownership that puts retailing into the domain of service processing. In fact, some manufacturing operations consist of a sequence of services applied to a physical object or system. Another physical attribute is location, and an operation that provides components to a just-in-time production process is a form of service.

### Information Processing Services

Information processing services deal with the collection, manipulation, interpretation, and transmission of data to create value for the client. Accounting, banking, consulting, education, insurance, legal, and news are commonly experienced examples of information processing services. There are important issues with information processing services, such as representation (as with lawyers and accountants), infrastructure (as with computers, databases, and the Internet), and self service (as with online facilities, ATM machines, and other administrative functions). This type of service is covered in a separate chapter, later in the book.

## CHARACTERISTICS OF SERVICES

In spite of the prevalence of services in everyday life, the subject is rarely considered and seldom defined. In business, services are commonly referred to as the non-material equivalent of a good. Services can be sold, purchased, and scheduled. To many people, a service represents something they cannot do themselves or do not want to do, or perhaps more importantly, something that can be done more efficiently or in a less costly manner by a specialized business entity. In fact, the agricultural and manufacturing sectors of the economy employ services, and the service sector also uses services. That said, exactly what constitutes a service is still up in the air, and a summary of the major definitive characteristics is certainly in order.

*A service is a process*. This notion is paramount to recognizing the far-reaching importance of service science as an academic discipline. A service takes input and produces output. In between the input and the output, there exist one or more steps that constitute the service process. Consider a simple medical example. A patient – the client – perceives a situation that requires attention. A contact with a medical provider is made and an appointment is scheduled for a service event. In general, the following three items of information are brought to the service process: the patient per se, a medical history, and the relevant information for the current problem. This is the client/customer input required for a service process. The physician performs the requisite consultation, diagnosis, and resolution that collectively constitute the service process. The output then consists of the diagnosis, prescription, prognosis, and update of the medical records. Additionally, the personal knowledge bases of the patient and physician are enhanced as a result of the service event.

*A service is heterogeneous.* This characteristic reflects the fact that each client/provider interaction in the form of a service event is unique. Some researchers refer to this characteristic as the fact that services are customized, either by design or by happenstance. Each service query to an information system or each instance of personal service, for example, is inherently different.

*A service captures value.* A service event creates a benefit to both the client and the provider, in the form of a change of state that is reflected in their physical condition or location, a change in their possessions, or in their assets. A service provider brings one or more of the following elements to the table: specific knowledge of the problem and solution domains, the time necessary to perform the service event, the physical wherewithal to perform the service event, and the requisite tools and equipment to perform the service event. Note that a location or infrastructure is not required since it may be associated with the client. The client provides the service object (i.e., the object or entity to which the service is applied) and necessary information, as required. The provider captures value through the execution of the service process. The client captures value as a result of the service process.

*A service cannot be inventoried.* The notion of opportunity loss is fundamental to service science. An empty seat on an airline flight cannot be resold. The value lost to a service provider due to a missed appointment cannot be regained. This characteristic gives a time dimension to services. Clearly, there are other flights and other appointments, but the time assigned to the execution of a service process is lost forever once the service window has closed. Thus, a service capacity is said to be *perishable*, referring to the fact that it is "perished" when unused.

*A service is intangible.* Although this characteristic was alluded to above, it deserves special attention because the definition of service products by the government uses the notion of a "change in the condition of a person or object" as the basis for classification. Services, especially in the areas of education and government, often result in social goods that are expressed in economic terms as hidden costs or opportunity costs.

*A service is consumed at the point of production.* This characteristic adds specificity to the recognition that a service is a process, even though it may be summarized for descriptive purposes as a service event. When a service terminates, it is finished. After the final step in a service process, the event is archived along with the consequent change of states of the client and provider.

*A service cannot be resold or given away.* It is not possible to pass a service on to another economic entity. The result of a service event is unique to that event, although information gained during the service process could theoretically be used by another entity. However, information resulting from a service event is not the same as the service event, because of the consumption characteristic.

*A service is co-produced.* This characteristic emphasizes the fact that because of the simultaneity of client and provider participation and the fact that a service event does not result in the production of a good, but rather in the state of something, it is commonly referred to as the co-production of value in the sense that if either of the participants were not present for the service event, it could not be interpreted as being a service.

An interesting question remains. Do the above characteristics uniquely reflect that a service is a process? There are two conditions: necessity and sufficiency[3]. If a service process must possess a characteristic to be classified as a service, then that characteristic is a necessary condition. However, possessing a necessary characteristic does not guarantee that the entity involved is a service, because there may be other such characteristics. On the other hand, if a process possessing a given characteristic is thereby automatically classified as a service, then it is regarded as a sufficient condition.

## SUMMARY

The subject of services is important to most people because they are employed in services and are also consumers of services. In the year 2000, U.S. service employment comprised 80% of the workforce. Surprisingly, very little attention is given to the service sector, in spite of the fact that most of us work in it.

A *service* is a provider/client interaction that creates and captures value. A unique characteristic of services, unlike agriculture and manufacturing, is that both parties participate in the transaction, and in the process, both capture value. In a sense, the provider and the client co-produce the service event, because one can't do without the other.

Services are generally classified by at least five criteria, although one criterion dominates. The minor factors are degree of provider labor intensity, degree of customer interaction, level of provider knowledge, and the amount

---

[3] See Sampson and Froehle (2006) p. 331.

of client information, that are quantitative measures brought to a service event. The major factor is a qualitative attribute known as "service nature," consisting of a service object and a service result. The focus is on the service object in this chapter, because it reflects whether a service is performed on a person, a possession, or information.

There are several definitive characteristics of services. They are summarized as follows. A service is a process. A service is heterogeneous. A service captures value. A service cannot be inventoried. A service is intangible. A service is consumed at the point of production. A service cannot be resold or given away. And finally, a service is co-produced.

## KEY TERMINOLOGY

The reader should be familiar with the following terms in the context in which they were used in the chapter.

| | |
|---|---|
| Client | Possession |
| Co-production | Processing |
| Heterogeneous | Provider |
| Information processing | Service bundle |
| Intangible | Service |
| Inventoried | Service package |
| Non-storable | Value proposition |
| People processing | |

## A FEW GOOD QUESTIONS[4]

1) Today, most of us are employed in _____.

2) A *service* is a provider/client interaction that creates and captures _____ _____.

3) Service activity is characterized by the fact that the results are usually ___ _____, meaning in this case that an artifact of some sort is not produced as a result of a service experience.

---

[4] Answers: (1) services; (2) value; (3) intangible; (4) co-produce; (5) quality; (6) people, possession, information.

4) In a sense, the provider and the client _____ the service event, because one can't do without the other.

5) With services, the client's view of _____ is generated during the service process.

6) Services are normally classified as _____ processing, _____ processing, and _____ processing.

## SELECTED READING

Friedman, T.L., *The Lexus and the Olive Tree*, New York: Anchor Books, 2000.

Friedman, T.L., *The World is Flat: A Brief History of the Twenty-First Century*, New York: Farrar, Straus and Giraux, 2006.

Harvard Business Review, *Business Value of IT*, Boston: Harvard Business School Press, 1999.

IBM Almaden Services Research, "SSME: What are services?" http://almaden.ibm.com/ssme, 2006.

Katzan, H., *A View of Service Science*, Southeast Decision Science Institute, Savannah, GA, February 21-23, 2007.

Maglio, P. and J. Zysman, *Toward a Science of Service Systems*, Sofcon 2007, Carnegie Mellon University, April 30, 2007, pp. 5-6.

Malone, T.W., *The Future of Work*, Boston: Harvard Business School Press, 2004.

Sampson, S.E. and C.M. Froehle, "Foundations and Implications of a Proposed Unified Services Theory," *Production and Operations Management*, Vol. 15, No. 2 (Summer, 2006), pp. 329-343.

# 2

# Service Models

A service is a socially designed and constructed form of activity in which a provider and a client collaborate to create social value. This chapter introduces the notion of socially constructed knowledge and then moves on to describe classes of services that are the building blocks of service systems. For the most part, we are straightforwardly classifying services that currently exist, so we can refer to them with some degree of sophistication. However, with the ontology we develop, it will be clear how service systems can be designed and created in the future. The methodology essentially provides an association between services, service models, service systems, and service innovation.

## SOCIAL CONSTRUCTIONISM

Social constructionism is the theory of knowledge based on the social and material setting in which a phenomenon is produced. In social constructionism, individuals and groups collaborate to create knowledge referred to as the philosophical doctrine of Equal Validity. Equal validity suggests that other means of knowing exist in addition to scientific facts. Consider three examples: the game of baseball, a baseball bat, and a five-cent coin. None but the hardened skeptic would deny knowledge about the three examples is a valid form of knowledge. Clearly, baseball is an activity developed by humans that has evolved into a non-trivial game of strategy. Knowledge about baseball is socially developed knowledge, not factual knowledge about something discovered through scientific research. A baseball bat, on the other hand, is constructed from wood that we as a society have discovered, not created, and would exist without the game of baseball and the social setting in which it exists. The precise form and substance of the bat is, however, another socially constructed form of knowledge, because it is something we have developed. So it is with the five-cent coin that represents more in a societal setting than the chemical elements of which it is constructed.

Accordingly, service systems are socially constructed forms of interaction wherein entities exchange beneficial forms of action through the combination of people and technologies that adapt to the changing level of information in the system. As such, reality constructed through social mechanisms is a dynamic process re-produced and maintained by social interactions. When persons interact, as in the execution of a service event, their shared perceptions of truth are reinforced as part of an objective reality.

The theory of social constructionism will be useful, later in the chapter, for the development of service models.

# CONCEPTS, CLASSES, AND SERVICE EVENTS

The basic question underlying services is, "Where do they come from?" It would appear that one entity simply makes up a service and another entity pays for it – in one way or another – when that service is engaged. As we shall see, it is more complicated than that. It is important to recall at this point that an entity can be a person, group, organization, and so forth, as long as the client entity can interact with the provider entity to create the mutual values to which we have referred previously. Both entities bring something to the service event and receive something when that activity has been completed.

## *The Notion of a Service Model*

Since service is socially-created phenomena, then some "needs" research must take place in order to create a template for the corresponding service event. At an elementary level, a service template is formed through a commonly-used innovation technique known as observational research. On the other hand, it may result from extensive research and testing in a laboratory established for that purpose. Regardless, the service template, which we will refer to as a "service model," must come from somewhere. For example, a physician/patient interaction and a visit to the hair dresser are one type of service, whereas lawn mowing and car detailing are another. In the former case, the service is performed on the client, whereas in the latter, the service is performed on a possession of the client. Similarly, when persons go to the Internet to obtain some information, they are also engaging in a service event. In this instance, there are some computers involved with the service along with a network, such that an Internet information system is the service provider. The object of their activity is the access to information managed by the Internet service provider and owned by the provider, client, or a third party.

To determine where a service comes from, we have to bring into play the notion of a concept and also restrict our thinking to a certain area of awareness. Philosophers would refer to the domain of investigation as a theory or a model of the universe. We can view the process as one of viewing the world through a special lens so that we only see what we are interested in. Within this special world, we develop concepts that eventually lead to classes of service.

## Concepts

A *concept* is an abstract idea or mental representation that facilitates the recognition of and reference to objects in a specific area of interest. Concepts are important because they allow us to omit the differences between things by abstracting their common characteristics. Thus, a concept is a mental phenomenon that allows us to identify and develop objects and processes in our world. Accordingly, we can easily conceptualize an elementary school as a place where boys and girls learn to read and write. Other tangible objects that are commonly conceptualized are automobiles, dogs, persons, and ball pens. The notion of a concept additionally applies to roles, processes, relationships, and events – to give only a few examples. The concept of a doctor refers to a person who gives medical advice without being very specific about that person. In early civilization, that label was given to anyone who assumed the role of giving medical advice – such as a village pharmacist. Similarly, the concept of learning refers to the process of acquiring knowledge. Other common concepts are marriage (as a relationship) and a ball game (as an event).

## Service Classes and Events

Concepts lead to classes that lead to objects. A *class* is a material representation of a concept and an *object* is an instance of a class. Stated differently, objects with common characteristics are grouped into a class and are represented by a concept. We can work backwards from object to concept because we are dealing with socially constructed phenomena. Here is a *hypothetical* example from the personal services domain:

*Service Universe*: Services performed on a person
*Service Concept*: Medical provisioning
*Service Class*: Physician/patient
*Service Event*: Individual visit to the doctor

In this instance, the service model is "physician/patient" conceptualized as medical provisioning within the service universe "services performed on a person." Here is another *hypothetical* service model:

*Service Universe*: Services performed on a possession of a person or an organization
*Service Concept*: Custodial provisioning
*Service Class*: Office maintenance
*Service Event*: Daily off-hours cleaning of executive suite

The service model is "office maintenance" conceptualized as custodial provisioning within the service universe "services performed on a possession of a person or an organization."

## Multiplicity of Service Classes in a Service Universe

Clearly, a given universe would engender many concepts that in turn would lead to multiple classes of service. In medical provisioning, for example, Physician/patient and Dentist/patient reflect different forms of medical service. (The names of service models and service concepts are capitalized to identify formal entities.) Service characteristics, such as these, delimit the extent of service models.

## Service Models and Specificity

Because services are socially developed phenomena, differing levels of specificity are needed to satisfy the requirements of a given situation. Consider the concept of a teacher and two instances: kindergarten and college professor. The roles are so diverse that a service model would be expected for each. On the other hand, consider laundry service and dry cleaning. In this case, a single service model would be sufficient because both instances originate from a similar underlying conceptual structure.

## Service Attributes

Objects are usually distinguished by their attributes, and classified by the same or different attributes. For example, if auto #1 is a red Buick and auto #2 is a blue Buick, then the two objects are distinguished by their color (red or blue) and classified by their brand name (Buick). Color and brand name are referred to as attributes. To continue, if auto # 3 is a red Ford and auto # 4 is a blue Ford, then auto # 1 (the red Buick) and # 3 (the red Ford), could be classified by their red color attribute, as red cars. It follows that attributes of services are used in the same manner to establish the boundaries of their corresponding service models. Incidentally, the notion of a red car is an example of a concept, as covered above.

Given this view of the classification of objects, it is now possible to be more definitive about the characteristics of services that were introduced in the first chapter.

## Service Dimensions

Accepting the fact that a service universe engenders service concepts that engender service classes that engender service events, where do the service universes come from? The question would be something that Socrates might have asked 2500 years ago. IBM Almaden Services Research and Fitzsimmons and Fitzsimmons have identified five dimensions along which we can classify services:

VI. *Service Process* – using the degrees of Customer Interaction and Customization (by the provider) and Provider Judgment or Labor Intensity as metrics

VII. *Service Nature* – using the Service Object and Service Result as metrics

VIII. *Service Delivery* – using Service Scheduling and Service Mode (continuous or discrete) as metrics

IX. *Service Availability* – using Service Site and Service Execution (who travels – provider or client) as metrics

X. *Service Demand* – using Demand Fluctuation and Service Capacity as metrics

We can use the five dimensions as service model generators.

## Service Process

Each dimension can be conceptualized as one view of a class of service models, and collectively, the six dimensions define a service universe. It is useful to think of the service universe as a point of view regarding the multiplicity of services that exist in a socially-constructed world. The Service Process dimension is employed as an introductory example.

Here is how it works. Each dimension can be viewed as a matrix, such as the following for Service Process[5]:

| | | Customer Interaction and Customization | |
|---|---|---|---|
| | | Low | High |
| Provider Judgment and Labor Intensity | Low | Airline Hotel | Hospital Auto Repair |
| | High | Retail School | Doctor Lawyer |

Each quadrant suggests a different service model, and the contents of that quadrant are examples of that type of service arrangement. Clearly, this is a very good start to defining classes of service, but there are a few open items, such as the specification of the service object on which the service is performed. Accordingly, the Service Process is a necessary condition but not a sufficient condition for defining a service model.

The service metrics deserve some consideration. The *Customer Interaction and Customization* metric refers to the degree of specific attention given by the provider to the client during the entire service event. When a client engages an airline seat or a hotel room, the facility is one of a select few possibilities and only a requisite amount of service is given to the client afterwards. With hospital service or auto repair, the service is unique to each client. The *Provider Judgment or Labor Intensity* metric can refer to three possibilities: (1) The amount of time the client receives attention when in the service process; and (2) The amount of time the provider is giving service when in the service process; and (3) The level of knowledge the provider

---

[5] The service diagrams in the IBM report are adapted from Fitzsimmons and Fitzsimmons (see selected readings).

brings to the service event. The service metrics are not precise in all cases; but it should be noted that our ultimate objective is to identify classes of service and not describe specific service events. (This comment will apply to other service dimensions, as well.)

## Service Nature

In order to achieve a greater degree of specificity, we can supplement the Service Process dimension with a Service Nature dimension, as follows[6]:

| | | Service Object | | |
|---|---|---|---|---|
| | | *People* | *Possession* | *Information* |
| Service Result | Tangible | Doctor Restaurant | Package transport Dry cleaning | Web search email |
| | Intangible | Media Education | Banking Insurance | Credit score Reputation |

Taking the services of a medical physician as an example, the service would be classified as follows:

| | |
|---|---|
| Service Process: | Provider Judgment or Labor Intensity (high), Client Interaction and Customization (high) |
| Service Nature: | Service Result (tangible), Service Object (people) |

As before, the characterizations of a physician's services to this point represent necessary conditions, but still not sufficient conditions. We need the additional dimensions for a complete classification.

The service metrics for the dimension Service Nature should be mentioned. The *Service Object* metric refers to the object on which the service is performed, whether it is a person or a possession belonging to a service entity. Recall that if the service object is information, it would belong to the possession category. The *Service Result* metric can refer to two possibilities: (1) In the case of a person

---

[6] *Op cit.* The remaining service matrices are introduced in the IBM report previously cited.

object, it refers to whether the service affects a person's physical presence, or it affects a person's mind; and (2) If the service object is a possession, it refers to whether the result is something one can usually observe.

## Service Delivery

The Service Delivery dimension reflects Service Scheduling and Service Mode (discrete or continuous) as follows:

| | | *Service Scheduling* | |
|---|---|---|---|
| | | *Formal* | *Informal* |
| *Service Mode* — Continuous | | Auto repair Insurance | Radio/TV Police |
| *Service Mode* — Discrete | | Doctor Hair dresser | Pay phone Restaurant |

The Service Delivery dimension reflects whether the provider specifically knows the client or schedules the service in advance (Service Scheduling) and whether the service has specific start and stop times or is a form of continuous service (Service Mode). Continuing with the physician example, we can specify the nature of the service with three dimensions as follows:

| | |
|---|---|
| Service Process: | Provider Judgment or Labor Intensity (high), Client Interaction and Customization (high) |
| Service Nature: | Service Result (tangible), Service Object (people) |
| Service Delivery: | Service Scheduling (formal), Service Mode (discrete) |

Clearly, there are edge cases in this form of analysis, but the design is sufficiently precise to delineate a Service Universe.

## Service Availability

The dimension of Service Availability specifies the Service Site where a service event is executed and which entity in the service relationship travels to affect the service (Service Execution), as follows:

|  | | Service Site | |
|---|---|---|---|
|  | | *Single* | *Multiple* |
| **Service Execution** | Provider Client Travels | Doctor Theatre | Fast food Bus service |
|  | Provider Travels | Taxi Pest control | Mail delivery Appliance repair |
|  | No Travel | Utilities Cell phone | Internet service |

This dimension gives evidence as to where a service takes place and the manner in which the service is arranged

Continuing with the physician example, we can specify the nature of the service with four dimensions as follows:

| Service Process: | Provider Judgment or Labor Intensity (high), Client Interaction and Customization (high) |
| Service Nature: | Service Result (tangible), Service Object (people) |
| Service Delivery: | Service Scheduling (formal), Service Mode (discrete) |
| Service Availability: | Service Site (single site), Service Execution (client travels) |

It is evident at this point that a service model for medical provisioning is clearly beginning to unfold.

## Service Demand

Service Demand refers to the degree to which demand for service fluctuates and the capacity of the service provider to satisfy variation in client needs for service:

| | | Demand Fluctuation | |
|---|---|---|---|
| | | *Wide* | *Narrow* |
| *Service Capacity* | *Flexible* | Utilities Police | Insurance Banking |
| | *Not Flexible* | Hotel Airline | Doctor Theatre |

Service Demand is a composite dimension because it reflects the degree of client demand and the capacity of the service provider to respond to demand changes. In a limited sense, demand fluctuation is always predictable. For example, doctor visits are usually up after a holiday or a weekend because people have an opportunity to think about their ills. However, the real question relates to peak demand and the flexibility inherent in service delivery. Some services can manage demand by scheduling and manage capacity by hiring part-time employees. Service Demand applied to the physician example yields the following list:

| | |
|---|---|
| Service Process: | Provider Judgment or Labor Intensity (high), Client Interaction and Customization (high) |
| Service Nature: | Service Result (tangible), Service Object (people) |
| Service Delivery: | Service Scheduling (formal), Service Mode (discrete) |
| Service Availability: | Service Site (single site), Service Execution (client travels) |
| Service Demand: | Demand Fluctuation (narrow), Service Capacity (not flexible) |

The physician example is complete in the sense that we have created a conceptual view of a medical provisioning service along the five dimensions.

## Epilogue to the Service Dimensions

It is important to recognize that a service model is not normative in any sense of the word. As an example, it doesn't tell you whether to go to a physician or a chiropractor. It doesn't tell you how to combine services or develop a service system. A service model defines one point in a five dimensional Cartesian space representing classes of services. What about service innovation? Simply go to a point in the space that is not represented and there is your innovation. There is, of course, much more to service innovation, but this is the basic idea.

# THE DNA OF SERVICES

The previous section introduced the notion of a five dimensional Cartesian space used to represent services and establish service models. An appropriate name for this space is a *service hyperspace*, because that is what it is. In this section, we are going to introduce how the service hyperspace can be used to uniquely define classes of service. The DNA of services[7] is used to delineate points in the service hyperspace.

## Characterization of the Service Matrices

It is useful to characterize the information inherent in a service matrix as a set of quadrants, as follows:

| | Column Metric | |
|---|---|---|
| Row Metric | A | B |
| | C | D |

and its cousin:

---

[7] In this instance, DNA is an acronym recursively defined as "DNA is Never Ambiguous."

**Column Metric**

|  | A | B |
|---|---|---|
| **Row Metric** | C | D |
|  | E | F |

Super imposing the set of quadrants on the Service Process matrix, for example, is reflected in the following diagram:

**Customer Interaction and Customization**

|  |  | Low | High |
|---|---|---|---|
| **Provider Judgment and Labor Intensity** | **Low** | Airline Hotel | Hospital Auto Repair |
|  | **High** | Retail School | Doctor Lawyer |

Quadrant A represents a *Low* value for the Customer Interaction and Customization (CIC) metric and a *Low* value for the Provider Judgment or Labor Intensity (PJL) metric. Similarly, quadrant D represents a *High* CIC value and a *High* PJL value, and so forth. The next step is to map the quadrants to a quadrant-based scale for representation in the service hyperspace.

### Quadrant-Based Scale

Continuing with the Service Process example, a service with *High* CIC and *Low* PJL values is given a value of B on the following quadrant-based scale:

| Low | A | B | C | D | High |
|---|---|---|---|---|---|
|  | Low CIC Low PJL | High CIC Low PJL | Low CIC High PJL | High CIC High PJL |  |

Table 2.1 gives the quadrant-based scales for the five dimensions in the service linear hyperspace. Each dimension has a quadrant-based scale based on the values for the associated metrics. Consider, for example, dimension #2 Service Nature. If the value for the Service Result metric is **Tangible** and the value for the Service Object metric is **Possession**, then the quadrant-based scale value for dimension #2 Service Nature is B.

Here is where the service DNA sequence comes in. Each service model has a unique DNA sequence, based on the quadrant-based scale values for each of its dimensions. Moreover, the various dimensions have an order based on the dimension numbers given in Table 2.1.

Recall the physician example given earlier in the chapter and summarized here:

| | |
|---|---|
| Service Process: | Provider Judgment or Labor Intensity (high), |
| | Client Interaction and Customization (high) |
| Service Nature: | Service Result (tangible), |
| | Service Object (people) |
| Service Delivery: | Service Scheduling (formal), |
| | Service Mode (discrete) |
| Service Availability: | Service Site (single site), |
| | Service Execution (client travels) |
| Service Demand: | Demand Fluctuation (narrow), |
| | Service Capacity (not flexible) |

From Table 2.1, dimension #1 (Service Process) has a DNA sequence value of D, because its value for the metric Provider Judgment or Labor Intensity is **High** and the value for the metric Client Interaction and Customization is also **High**. Similarly, dimension #2 (Service Nature) has a DNA sequence value of A, because its value for the metric Service Result is **Tangible** and the value for the metric Service Object is **People**. Using the same thinking, dimension #3 (Service Delivery) has a DNA sequence value of C; dimension #4 (Service Availability) has a DNA sequence value of A; and finally, dimension #5 (Service Demand) has a DNA sequence value of D. So the complete service DNA sequence for the physician model is DACAD.

## Additional Examples of Service DNA Sequences

The service customarily known as "lawn mowing" is represented by the following script:

| Service Process: | Provider Judgment or Labor Intensity (high), |
| | Client Interaction and Customization (low) |
| Service Nature: | Service Result (tangible), |
| | Service Object (possession) |
| Service Delivery: | Service Scheduling (formal), |
| | Service Mode (discrete) |
| Service Availability: | Service Site (single site), |
| | Service Execution (provider travels) |
| Service Demand: | Demand Fluctuation (narrow), |
| | Service Capacity (not flexible) |

The key attributes of this kind of service is that the provider travels and performs the service on a possession of the client. The labor intensity is high but the service is normally not customized for each client. The activity is scheduled and takes a finite time. The demand doesn't vary and the provider usually has a limited capacity to perform the service. The service DNA sequence for this service model is CBCCD.

Next, consider a "hotel" example, characterized as follows:

| Service Process: | Provider Judgment or Labor Intensity (low), |
| | Client Interaction and Customization (low) |
| Service Nature: | Service Result (tangible), |
| | Service Object (people) |
| Service Delivery: | Service Scheduling (formal), |
| | Service Mode (discrete) |
| Service Availability: | Service Site (single sites), |
| | Service Execution (client travels) |
| Service Demand: | Demand Fluctuation (wide), |
| | Service Capacity (not flexible) |

The key attributes in this example are that the client travels, customization is low, and the result is tangible because the client uses the hotel's facilities for a prescribed period of time. Clearly, the service object is people, the service is scheduled, and the activity is discrete. The service capacity is fixed even though there may be wide demand fluctuation. The service DNA sequence for this model is AACAC.

Dimension #1: ***Service Process***

| Provider Judgment/ Labor Intensity | Customer Interaction/ Customization | Quadrant-Based Scale |
|---|---|---|
| Low | Low | A |
| Low | High | B |
| High | Low | C |
| High | High | D |

Dimension #2: ***Service Nature***

| Service Result | Service Object | Quadrant-Based Scale |
|---|---|---|
| Tangible | People | A |
| Tangible | Possessions | B |
| Intangible | People | C |
| Intangible | Possessions | D |
| Tangible | Information | E |
| Intangible | Information | F |

Dimension #3: ***Service Delivery***

| Service Mode | Service Scheduling | Quadrant-Based Scale |
|---|---|---|
| Continuous | Formal | A |
| Continuous | Informal | B |
| Discrete | Formal | C |
| Discrete | Informal | D |

Dimension #4: ***Service Availability***

| Service Execution | Service Site | Quadrant-Based Scale |
|---|---|---|
| Client Travels | Single Site | A |
| Client Travels | Multiple Sites | B |
| Provider Travels | Single Site | C |
| Provider Travels | Multiple Sites | D |
| No Travel | Single Site | E |
| No Travel | Multiple Sites | F |

Dimension #5: ***Service Demand***

| Service Capacity | Demand Fluctuation | Quadrant-Based Scale |
|---|---|---|
| Flexible | Wide | A |
| Flexible | Narrow | B |
| Not Flexible | Wide | C |
| Not Flexible | Narrow | D |

***Table 2.1 Quadrant-Based Scales for the Five Dimensions in Service Hyperspace***

## Information Systems Service DNA Sequence

The service customarily known as a "web search" is represented by the following script:

| | |
|---|---|
| Service Process: | Provider Judgment or Labor Intensity (high), Client Interaction and Customization (low) |
| Service Nature: | Service Result (tangible), Service Object (information) |
| Service Delivery: | Service Scheduling (informal), Service Mode (discrete) |
| Service Availability: | Service Site (single site), Service Execution (no travel) |
| Service Demand: | Demand Fluctuation (wide), Service Capacity (flexible) |

The key attributes of this kind of service are that neither the client or provider travels, and the labor intensity is high, because sophisticated software is required, but the service is normally not customized for each client. The activity is not scheduled and takes a finite time. The demand varies widely and the provider usually has unlimited capacity to perform the service. The service DNA sequence for this information system service model is CEDEA.

# MODELS, CLASSES, AND OBJECTS

Each service model can be uniquely identified by a service DNA sequence. But, what if two models have the same DNA sequence? It could easily happen since many services have the same signature, as in the following examples:

Medical provisioning: doctor, dentist, chiropractor
Transportation: airline, bus
Home service: lawn mowing, gutter cleaning, window washing

If two service models have the same service DNA sequence, then they are in the same class, as defined previously. Recall, that the term "service model" is used in this chapter to represent a template for a class or an object – whatever is appropriate at the moment.

We can also construct a service DNA sequence representing a service class with no instances (i.e., objects). Because service systems are socially constructed forms of knowledge, we are not constrained by nature to describe only what exists. We can be innovative and design service systems to satisfy a variety of needs. Service systems are covered in the next chapter.

# SUMMARY

Service systems are socially constructed forms of interaction wherein entities exchange beneficial forms of action through the combination of people and technologies that adapt to the changing level of information in the system. Both entities – provider and client – bring something to the service event and receive something when that activity has been completed.

To determine where a service comes from, we have to bring into play the notion of a concept and also restrict our thinking to a certain area of awareness. We can view the process as one of viewing the world through a special lens so that we only see what we are interested in. Within this special world, we develop concepts that eventually lead to classes of service.

Concepts lead to classes that lead to objects. A *class* is a material representation of a concept and an *object* is an instance of a class. Objects are usually distinguished by their attributes, and classified by the same or different attributes.

Using service attributes, five service dimensions have been identified:

I. *Service Process* – using the degrees of Customer Interaction and Customization (by the provider) and Provider Judgment or Labor Intensity as metrics

II. *Service Nature* – using the Service Object and Service Result as metrics

III. *Service Delivery* – using Service Scheduling and Service Mode (continuous or discrete) as metrics

IV. *Service Availability* – using Service Site and Service Execution (who travels – provider or client) as metrics

V. *Service Demand* – using Demand Fluctuation and Service Capacity as metrics

The five dimensions are used as service model generators. A linear scale is developed so that a DNA of Services, based on the dimensions and the scale, is feasible. In the physician/patient model, for example, the service DNA sequence would be DACAD.

The service DNA sequence gives some options for service innovation.

# KEY TERMINOLOGY

The reader should be familiar with the following terms in the context in which they were used in the chapter.

Class
Collaborate
Concept
Equal validity
Object
Service availability
Service delivery
Service demand
Service DNA
Service model
Service nature
Service process
Service universe

## A FEW GOOD QUESTIONS[8]

1) A service is a socially designed and constructed form of activity in which a provider and a client _____ to create _____ _____.

2) In social constructionism, individuals and groups collaborate to create knowledge referred to as the philosophical doctrine of _____ _____.

3) A _____ is an abstract idea or mental representation that facilitates the recognition of and reference to objects in a specific area of interest.

4) A _____ is a material representation of a concept and an _____ is an instance of a class.

5) Give the five dimension in the service model: _____, _____, _____, _____, and _____.

6) An attribute of a service dimension is called a service _____ _____.

---

[8] Answers: (1) collaborate, social value; (2) Equal Validity; (3) concept; (4) class, object; (5) service process, service nature, service delivery, service availability, service demand; (6) metric.

# SELECTED READING

Fitzsimmons, J.A. and M.J. Fitzsimmons, *Service Management: Operations, Strategy, Information Technology* (5th Edition), New York: McGraw-Hill Irwin, 2006.

IBM Almaden Services Research, "SSME: What are services?"

http://almaden.ibm.com/ssme, 2006.

Martin, J. and J.J. Odell, Object-Oriented Methods: A Foundation (2nd Edition), Upper Saddle River, NJ: Prentice Hall PTR, 1998.

Sampson, S.E. and C.M. Froehle, *"Foundations and Implications of a Proposed Unified Services Theory,"* Production and Operations Management, Vol. 15, No. 2 (Summer, 2006), pp. 329-343.

# 3

# Service Systems

A *service system* is a collection of resources and economic entities, capable of engaging in or supporting one or more service events. The resources are the infrastructure and other facilities necessary to support the service process. The economic entities are the service provider and service client that co-produce the service event. In the case of possession processing services, the service environment would also consist of one or more tangible objects that serve as the service object of the service process. In this sense, the service object is referred to as the "*operand* of the service process." In most cases, a service system is required to sustain a service event. Figure 3.1 suggests a service system.[9] In this instance, the service target could be the client, a possession of the client, or an individual or an organizational entity over which the client has responsibility.

## SYSTEMS CONCEPTS

In its most general sense, a *system* is a set of objects with relationships between the objects and between their attributes. The objects are the

---

[9] Adapted from Maglio, P.P., *Service Science, Management, and Engineering (SSME): An Interdisciplinary Approach to Service Innovation*, IBM Almaden Research Center, http://almaden.ibm.com/ssme, p. 14.

components or parts of the system and are generally unlimited in scope and variety. In actual practice, however, the objects of which a system is synthesized give the system its structure and implicitly determine the practical limits on its functional operability. Attributes are the properties of objects, and the relationships connect the system together, so it can be regarded as a single entity.

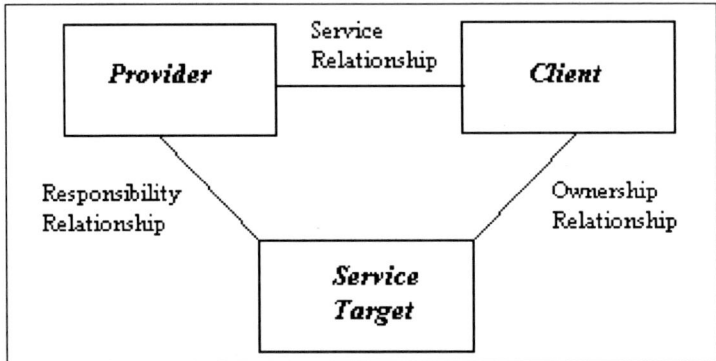

*Figure 3.1 Systems View of the Service Relationship*

## Relationships

A relationship can take the form of a physical connection, a logical similarity, a causal rule, and so forth. In a service system, a relationship is the service that the provider and the client co-produce. Neither a provider nor a client, by itself, is a service system. By definition, both entities are required, along with the relationship that takes the form of a service process.

## Environment

Systems usually exist with the support of an environment. The *environment* of a system exists as the objects outside of a system. The attributes of the outside objects determine whether the operation of the system is affected by those objects, or the outside objects are changed by the operation of the system.

## System Attributes

*Open systems* interface or exchange information with their environment; *closed systems* do not interface with their environment and there is no exchange between them. In the same manner that objects possess attributes, systems do also. Systems have been variously classed as being adaptive, probabilistic, deterministic, stable, and possessing a feedback mechanism. Service systems are almost always open systems because they require a nurturing environment in order to survive.

## Service Systems Ontology

The nature of the existence of a class of systems is referred to as a *systems ontology*, which establishes a distinction between real systems, conceptual systems, and abstract systems. The existence of *real systems* can be perceived or inferred by observation and exist independently of the observer. *Conceptual systems* utilize logical or mathematical constructs to model a system's operation. *Abstract systems* form a subset of conceptual systems and exist as conceptual systems with a real counterpart.

Service systems are real systems that are socially constructed, so that an appropriate ontology is encompassed by the following definition:

> The subject of *ontology* is the study of the *categories* of things that exist or may exist in some domain. The product of such a study, also called ontology, is a catalog of the types of things that are assumed to exist in a domain of interest *D* from the perspective of a person who uses the language *L* for the purpose of talking about *D*. The types in the ontology represent the *predicates, word senses,* or *concept and relation types* of the language *L* when used to discuss topics in the domain *D*.[10]

One common approach to the listing of ontological elements is to divide the entities into groups called *categories*. Each category is different from the others and has a descriptive of its own. It is in this latter sense that the service models, given in chapter two, serve as a basis for service systems.

## Reductionist View

In order to have a service, you need three basic things: a client, a provider, and a service process. Each is required to materialize a service event. You can have all the service providers in the world, but without a client and a relationship, there is no service. The same holds true for clients and relationships. Accordingly, a provider without a client and an appropriate service relationship is viewed as a nascent provider, or perhaps an unrealized provider.

---

[10] John F. Sowa (2000).

However, there is much more to a service system. In the next section, we concentrate on the infrastructure needed for the service. In later sections, we will focus on the service process.

# SERVICE PROVISIONING

If a service provider and client can co-produce a service event, there must be some degree of geographical locality to the situation, in the sense that the client travels to the provider or the provider travels to the client or the client and provider execute the service event in a third-party location or they communicate via some form of interactive device and its corresponding media. In other words, they have to get together.

## *The Service Facility*

First up, let's consider the case where the customer travels to facilities associated with the provider, such as an airline terminal, hospital, restaurant, retail establishment, or hotel – to name only a few examples. Furthermore, let's refer to the provider facilities as the *service factory*. The basic idea is that the customer remains at the service factory during service delivery.

The situation quickly gets complicated because it depends on whether or not the service is associated with a tangible object, an intangible object, or a production supply chain. A *pure service* is a service not associated with tangible objects, such as in medical treatment, hair coloring, and personal transportation. The service event is scheduled, initiated, terminated, and archived – all in the service factory. Many service processes are comprised of several steps called the *service chain*. Other services, not just pure services, consist of a service chain, but this characteristic is normally associated with pure services. When a service process consists of a service chain, it is said to be "scripted." Clearly, a service script may be implicit in the service, such as a doctor's visit, or it may be explicitly prescribed as part of a formal service agreement. Depending upon the complexity of the situation, services can also be a part of a goods production process or a conventional supply chain.

The notion of a service factory also applies to service events in which the client picks up a tangible object, or receives an object resulting from a production process, as when an airline ticket is purchased at an airline terminal. So, for example, a drive-up window at a fast food restaurant is categorized as a service factory, since the client is physically located at the service facility however short the time span of the service event. In this case, however, the pick-up service is associated with a production process that engenders the associated tangible object. The client obtains an object that is closely associated with the pick-up service, in contradistinction to the case, as covered in the next section, where the client brings in some artifact to a service shop for service and later picks it up.

A related consideration is whether the service is classified as being discrete or continuous. Hospital service is continuous consisting of a series of service events. Moreover, the service events may be dynamic in the sense that they are not necessarily planned beforehand. A doctor's visit, on the other hand, ordinarily consists of a service chain of planned events, wherein the services might include check in, get weighed, interact with the physician, and so forth.

Some continuous services, such as insurance and banking, incorporate a service factory that is closely associated with the provider but not the client. Clearly, services of this type have a service initiation, service agreements, and eventually a termination; but in-between service events are dynamic in the sense that they may occur on an unscheduled and unplanned basis.

Still other services in this category may utilize more than one service facility, such as a check-in terminal and a transportation vehicle. However, the classification applies since the client occupies provider facilities for the duration of the service. Branch banking is a form of continuous service with more than one service facility.

## The Service Shop

Secondly, some services involve leaving a possession of the client at a service shop for later pick-up, as in the cases of dry cleaning and auto repair. Clearly, the service shop is associated with the service provider, and it is the service object, owned by the client, that occupies physical space in the service facility for the duration of the service process.

## The Service Portal

Lastly, some services engage a virtual service facility for the duration of the service event. All of this sounds like the Internet, and that's the idea. However, the category also includes telecommuting and a variety of online and telephone services. In fact, any activity, generally classed as e-Commerce, falls under the umbrella of a service portal. Included in the category of service portals are a variety of information services and "do it yourself" activities.

An interesting phenomenon exists concerning the metaphorical conception of the World Wide Web (WWW). Maglio and Matlock[11] interviewed beginning and experienced web users and determined that people

---

[11]Maglio, P.P. and T. Matlock (1998), *Metaphors We Surf the Web By*, The Information Architecture Institute.

naturally think of the web as a physical space in which they move. So, even though the web is not physical, users – that is, clients in the service domain – conceptually travel to the service provider.

### Mobile Service Facilities

In the previous categories, the emphasis has been on provider resources that occupy a fixed space, incorporating personnel, buildings, equipment, machines, vehicles, and supplies. The scenario has been that the client travels to the service facility or accesses it via some modern convenience. There are also services wherein the provider travels to a third party location to perform a service for a client, such as the car washing. In this form of service, the provider travels to a location, such as a parking lot, where the service is performed. Various forms of road service additionally fall into this category.

In other cases, the client moves as in navigation services and various forms of satellite communication, such as radio, information providing, and related services – such as car unlocking.

### Client Facilities

The subject of service provisioning would not be complete without the mention of client facilities, as in the case where the service provider travels to the client to perform a service, such as personal training, lawn care, cleaning, landscaping, and so forth. In most instances in this group, the service is performed on a possession of the client – even though that is not a necessary condition.

## SERVICE IMPLEMENTATION

All organizations and all persons do not have the same service requirements, and accordingly, the same problems. Moreover, it is impossible to look at services from solely an industry perspective or even a personal point of view. Clearly, services differ between industries and between persons. On the other hand, the diverse set of activities universally called *services* wouldn't be called *services* if there weren't some degree of commonality among them. Accordingly, we are going to take a look at steps in the service process, not necessarily service interactions, per se, that are commonly incorporated into the service chain. Next, we will take a look at operations that are specific to a particular service. Table 3.1 gives a summary of the functions and operations in the general category of service organization.

| Generic Functions to Sustain a Service | Generic Operations to Achieve a Service |
|---|---|
| Service initiation<br>Entry administration<br>Service interactions<br>Service termination<br>Exit administration<br>Service archiving | Scheduling<br>Accept customer input<br>Perform services<br>Representation<br>Referral<br>Schedule auxiliary services<br>Schedule supplementary services |

*Table 3.1 Functions and operations in the general category of service organization.*

## Generic Functions Performed During Service

It is necessary and important to emphasize the difference between generic functions performed to sustain a service – any service – and specific operations performed to achieve a service. In the former case, we are dealing with steps that support a service process including: initiation, entry administration, sustains service interactions, termination, exit administration, and archiving. Some of the functions are not present in all services, or they are implicit in an informal service arrangement. In most cases, the generic functions necessary for sustaining services can be viewed as organizational activities.

Service *initiation* refers to the steps necessary to schedule a service and establish a provider/client interaction. Appointments with professional service providers are normally scheduled, whereas arrangements with nonprofessionals are commonly scheduled on an informal basis. Some service providers use appointments to manage demand as a means of achieving service efficiency. Entry service *administration* initiates customer input, such as filling out forms, and establishes a service agreement encompassing fees and expectations. Legal documents may be involved with this step, and client requirements are delineated. Service *interactions* are the steps in the service process. For discrete service processes, service interactions are statically planned with expected variations, since most services are customized by the provider for each client. For continuous service processes, service interactions are dynamically engaged – as in the case of banking, insurance, and hospital care. Service *termination* represents the end of a set of service interactions, regardless if they are statically or dynamically executed. Follow-on services or referrals are established during this step. Exit service *administration* initiates the record-keeping process and deals with the economic aspects of the service process. Service *archiving* handles information storage and legal requirements.

Collectively, the six generic functions are normally present, explicitly or implicitly, in practically all service processes, and are referred to as the *service platform*. The intended meaning of the terminology is that the service platform supports the service process.

## Generic Operations Performed to Achieve Service

The operations performed to achieve a particular service using a service platform for support are summarized in Table 3.1. Most, if not all, operations performed in a service environment can easily be mapped to the seven generic operations given. *Scheduling* refers to demand management. *Customer input* represents the collaboration and information exchange portion of a service event. The entry identified as "perform services" is the subset of the service chain peculiar to a particular form of service. *Referral* is the stage in some forms of consultation where the client is directed to another service provider for more definitive service. *Representation* denotes a step in the service chain where the service provider, or an associate, represents the client in some form of negotiation. Two noteworthy examples of representation are in legal or tax service. *Auxiliary services* represent tasks performed to support the primary service function, such as taking blood for a physical examination. *Supplementary services* are activities such as billing, financing, and reporting – operations that are not directly part of the primary service function. A couple of examples will demonstrate this point of view.

The traditional operations performed in banking are teller activity, check clearing, transaction processing, record keeping, vault operations, treasury operations, security, and maintenance. Teller activity, transaction processing, and record keeping are associated with scheduling, customer input, and service performance. The other banking operations, customarily known as back-office operations easily map to supplementary and auxiliary service.

Another example is airline service. The traditional airline functions are customer support and ticketing, ground support, ground operations, and flight operations that easily correspond to scheduling, customer input, service performance, and auxiliary operations.

Traditional law office operations present a good example of diversity since the commonly known operations of scheduling, consultation, research, reporting and representation readily correspond to the given generic operations.

# BUSINESS SERVICE SYSTEMS

The basis of business service systems is the evolution from collaboration to automation, as suggested by Figure 3.2.[12] The first phase, entitled *Collaboration*, utilizes human engineering principles and is characterized as "assistance by doing some of the work." The next phase, entitled *Augmentation*, utilizes technology to increase productivity by using tools to supplement human activity. The third phase, entitled *Delegation*, is the outsourcing to service providers of non-core business processes that do not provide competitive advantage. The final phase, entitled *Automation*, employs technology to provide self-service systems. Employing the four elements of business service systems, namely organization, technology, management, and information systems, service businesses can move among the phases by considering the following elements: business value (*Should we?*), technology (*Can we?*), governance (*May we?*), and business priorities (*Will we?*).

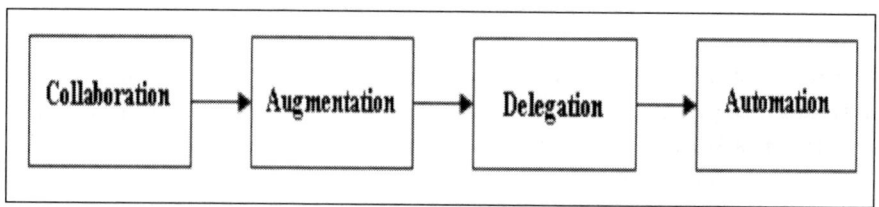

***Figure 3.2 Evolution of Business Service Systems.***

## *Globalization*

A business service system is a complex socio-techno-economic system[13] that combines people, technology, value, and clients along four dimensions:[14] information sharing, work sharing, risk sharing, and goods sharing. There is some evidence that some elements of all four dimensions are present in all business service systems. Before globalization, services were performed between provider and client with some degree of locality. After Globalization Three[15], business value creation through services is created by sharing. Information and communications technology (ICT) is the key business

---

[12] Adapted from *Service Science, Management, and Engineering (*SSME): Challenges, Frameworks, and Call for Participation*, IBM Almaden Research Center, http:// almaden.ibm.com/ssme, p. 13.

[13] Maglio (2007) op cit. p. 22.

[14] Maglio and Spohrer (2007), p.4.

[15] Friedman, T.L. (2006), p. 10.

driver in value creation and is the form of technology most closely aligned with business service systems.

## Information and Communications Technology

ICT is the latest in a long chain of buzzwords intended to refer to what business, government, and education do with computers. The most interesting implication of the acronym ICT, however, is that the availability of computers and communications to do just about any digital job we can think of is taken for granted. In a real sense, it is the application of technology to the co-creation of value by the interaction of provider and client, without requiring that the service participants be in the same location.

An information system is a collection of hardware, software, databases, telecommunications facilities, people, and operational procedures designed to collect, manipulate, store, process, and communicate data among components of an enterprise. An information system, sometimes known as a computer-based information system, is a service provider and its clients are the people, employees, business partners, and even other information systems in that application domain. As a multidimensional service provider, an information system is a platform for the nationalization and globalization of services. The effect of ICT is not restricted to information alone. Through ICT, multinational supply chains, to give only one example, are not only possible, but desirable.

The effectiveness of ICT is, of course, directly related to the Internet, because it lowers the cost of operating on a national and international scale. Consumers and enterprises alike can operate in a global marketplace to obtain lower costs for goods and services on a 24/7 schedule. Clearly, low-cost suppliers and service providers are available globally. The use of ICT in service provisioning is more closely associated with business services than it is with personal and domestic services.

## Business Agility

Businesses operating digitally through ICT can leverage time and space globally to better respond to market demands. An agile firm is one that achieves responsiveness by allowing work to proceed continuously (*time management*) and at multiple international locations (*space management*).

## Outsourcing

*Outsourcing* is the transfer of the ownership of a business process to a supplier, which includes management and day-to-day execution of that function.[16]   The most commonly outsourced business processes are information technology, human resources, accounting, customer support, and call center operations.   The key characteristics of outsourcing are "transfer" and ownership; it is different from the process in which the buyer retains control and tells the supplier how to do the work.   The objective of outsourcing can be and often is one of the following: reducing costs, focusing the capability of a particular business on more profitable activities, and to obtain special capabilities that the provider firm may possess.   Core business competencies are usually not outsourced.   For example, airlines commonly outsource telephone reservation and information systems to foreign companies in order to reduce costs and focus on flight operations.   Another example, more close to home, is the outsourcing of business cleaning services to benefit from economies of scale for that type of service.

With outsourcing, the client and the provider enter into a business relationship, established with a substantial business agreement, and then the service provider takes over the business process.   Outsourcing is usually – actually, almost always – associated with offshoring, but that need not necessarily be the case.

## Offshoring

*Offshoring* is a general term that describes the relocation of a business process from one country to another.[17]   Although the present context is services, the practice also applies to manufacturing and production.   If a country can provide services in a less expensive manner than other countries, it gives them a comparative advantage to freely trade those services.   In the modern world of ICT for the appropriate services, therefore, offshoring can be achieved by establishing the necessary business ecosystem.

To be more specific, offshoring is the practice[18] of transferring an internal business process of a company in one country to another country, to be executed by the same or a different company.   Service offshoring is particularly appealing to modern business since many services can be digitized thereby facilitating inter-country relocation.

---

[16] Wikipedia gives a good description of **outsourcing** along with a comprehensive list of references and links.

[17] Wikipedia gives a good description of **offshoring** along with a comprehensive list of references and links.

[18] Use of the term "practice" is by intension.   It is meant to denote that the process is prevalent.

Offshoring may involve the transfer of intellectual property and training to the receiving country and is related to the availability of educated and trained labor as factors in production – the others being land and capital. Accordingly, many design and development services have been redirected offshore.

## Outsourcing and Offshoring

It follows from the above discussion that a company that engages in the transfer of an entire business function to another company in another country is both outsourcing and offshoring. As mentioned previously, common examples of outsourcing are call centers, accounting, customer support, human relations, and information technology (IT). It is now appropriate to add medical diagnosis, design services, and engineering services to the list and recognize that both outsourcing and offshoring are involved.

Public opinion on combined outsourcing and offshoring (O&O) is negative, because it is generally felt that the process adversely affects individuals and the total labor market. Even in cases in which O&O is associated with lower jobless rates, it is felt that O&O tends to shift displaced workers into lower paying jobs.

## Transformational Outsourcing

Many executives feel that outsourcing allows the firm to concentrate on core competencies and, in the case of ICT, achieve greater flexibility. Because many business processes are totally dependant upon computers, business agility is necessary for developing responsiveness in the marketplace. *Transformational outsourcing* refers to the combination of cost saving with the potential for strategic flexibility and supplements cost focus with opportunity focus.

The underlying idea is that through transformational outsourcing, the firm will be transformed into one with the requisite characteristics. Innovation in supplying services is required, therefore, because services are almost always customized and are labor intensive. Moreover, competition in the services marketplace does not tend to drive down process and profit margins.

The key point, of course, is that outsourced services do not usually provide differentiation in the marketplace.

## Sharing

The major tenet of services is that the provider and the client co-produce a service event and the composite interaction creates value for both of the participants. To a greater or lesser degree, a service is enacted by sharing, as covered previously.[19] Information sharing is more closely aligned with services in which persons interact, such as medical provisioning and consulting. Work sharing is characterized by outsourcing. Risk sharing (although not covered so far) is associated with continuous form of service, such as insurance, and is related to transformational outsourcing. Goods sharing is involved with certain formal tangible people-oriented services, such as hotel and auto rental.

### Composite Services

It is conceivable that a firm will want to transfer certain in-house operations to another country to reduce costs and take advantage of specific labor conditions. This process, sometimes known as FDI, or Foreign Direct Investment, allows the firm to maintain control while achieving the aforementioned benefits. From that point, it is a short step from inside offshoring to outside offshoring.

Another outsourcing possibility is to transfer equipment and personnel to the supplier, along with the business process, as in the case of some companies that transferred their total ICT operations to an outside company. Many people feel, however, that the transferred personnel have a lower level of job security in their new employment habitat.

Finally, chapter one covered the case where services exist at two or more levels, as in the airline example. In this example, the outsourced and offshored service company enters into a service agreement with the airline to deliver information and reservation services to passengers. In this instance, the service provider has two clients: the airline and the passengers, with no stake in the eventual outcome except as governed in the service level agreement. Service packages in this category have serious drawbacks in the area of service quality and customer retention.

## SERVICE PROCESS ORGANIZATION

Practically everyone has heard of or experienced service providers that traditionally have clients backed up with very long waiting times.[20] Another common example is the "not so fast" fast-food restaurant. In the world of services, organization is everything.

---

[19] Maglio and Spohrer (2007), *ibid.*

[20] You guessed it; it is the family doctor. But things have changed dramatically in recent years.

## Expectations

While it is literally impossible to solve all service problems in a few pages, it is feasible to deliver an organizational design that is relevant to most service systems. Recall the definition of a service system:

> A *service system* is a system of people and technology that adapts to the changing value of information in the system.

It is important to emphasize that the "changing value of information" also refers to the service process itself. In other words, know thyself.[21] So it should be expected that a particular service organization would adjust to changing conditions in the workplace.

In the production of goods, a measure of organization is the level of inventory, even though the management of inventory can be a subject in its own right. With services, capacity is key, and long waiting lines are evidence of insufficient service capacity, ineffective demand management, or inadequate organization.

In this section, a working model of service organization is presented that should serve as a starting point for looking at organizational issues.

## An Organization Example – Retailing and Services

The importance of service organization is inherent in retailing. Retailing is a service, as covered previously, and the sales service event changes the ownership attribute of a product. A significant aspect of retailing exists, however, that is associated with service organization.

There is a component in retailing that is directly related to the level of expected service as a function of the price of the product. Most customers possess a nominal price for a given product. If the sales price is lower than nominal value, then less service is expected. If the sales price is higher than the nominal price, then more service is expected or the product is deemed overpriced. Buyer behavior, therefore, is governed by a combination of price and retail service, so that buyer behavior is influenced to some degree by service organization.

## Service, Service Providers, and Service Process

Clearly, there is a difference between a service and its service provider. In doctoring, the service is the medical attention afforded the patient, and the

---

[21] A famous philosopher, namely Socrates, once emphasized those words.

46

service provider is the doctor. In auto maintenance and repair, the service provider is the dealership (assuming new car sales, adhering to the KISS principle)[22] and the service process is the well-known service event, involving the service advisor, service technician, and a whole host of other providers.

Accordingly, the *service process* in the following set of steps is the service chain, mentioned previously: service initiation, entry administration, service interactions, service termination, and service archiving. This is a generic set of steps, and each particular form of service has its own set of provisional operations. We will develop a service organization model based on the given generic service chain.

## *Up a Notch*

It is important to recognize that in covering the subject of service process organization, we are going up a level in service provisioning. Most forms of service go through a sequence of steps – a form of transitional services – where some of the steps are established by the service provider and are not part of the service event, per se.

The service organization model introduced here is called the "transitional service organization" and an auto service arrangement is used as an example.

## *Transitional Service Organization Model*

In a transitional form of service organization, the service process from the client's and service provider's viewpoints consists of the following steps. (1) The owner (client) makes an appointment for service with the appointment scheduler (the demand manager). (2) The client brings the car (service object) to the dealership for service. (3) The client interacts with the service advisor (service facilitator) to exchange service particulars. (4) The client waits for service or leaves the dealership's premises (the service factory). (5) The service arrangement is entered into a computer (the service scheduler) by the service facilitator. (6) The service technician (the server) subsequently picks up the service order and performs the required service, often coordinating with the service facilitator for additional information. (7) The server registers the service completion with the service scheduler. (8) The service scheduler sends a request to the service administrator for billing. (9) The client interacts with the service administrator for pickup and payment resolution and the service event is completed.

---

[22] KISS – Keep It Short and Simple, or its equivalent.

The service model consists of five key relationships: governance, information, service, ownership, and the service-level agreement. Additionally, there are nine major components: the service provider, the service client, the service manager, the service facilitator, the service scheduler, the service server, the service object, the demand manager, and the service administrator. Each element is considered in detail in a subsequent chapter on the business of services.

The model applies to the three major forms of service: people processing, possession processing, and information services, as covered in the next chapter.

## SUMMARY

A service system is a system of people and technology that adapts to the changing value of knowledge in the system. The participants in a service system are the provider and client and the relationship between them is the service process. Systems of this type require an environment in which to operate that can take the form of a service factory in which the client resides for the duration of the service process and the service shop in which a possession of the client resides for the duration of the service event.

Service systems are facilitated by information and communications technology and enhanced by globalization. Service provisioning is inherent in outsourcing and offshoring. Innovation in supplying services is required because services are usually customized and labor intensive.

Core business processes are not customarily outsourced, and outsourcing predominantly does not provide differentiation in the marketplace.

The transitional service organization model demonstrates the commonality and variability of service systems, and gives rise to three proposed laws of service systems.

## KEY TERMINOLOGY

The reader should be familiar with the following terms in the context in which they were used in the chapter.

Abstract system
Augmentation
Automation
Business agility
Categories
Closed system
Collaboration
Composite service

Conceptual system
Delegation
Environment (of a system)
ICT
Offshoring
Ontology
Open system
Outsourcing
Real system
Reductionist view
Service administration
Service archiving
Service factory
Service initiation
Service interaction
Service platform
Service portal
Service relationship
Service shop
Service system
Service termination
Space management
System
Time management
Transformational outsourcing

## A FEW GOOD QUESTIONS[23]

1) A _____ is a set of objects with relationships between the objects and their attributes.

2) ____ _____ interface or exchange information with their environment.

3) With a _____ _____, the customer remains at the facility during service delivery.

---

[23] Answers: (1) system; (2) open systems; (3) service factory; (4) service portal; (5) customer input; (6) collaboration, augmentation, delegation, automation; (7) outsourcing; (8) offshoring.

4)  As far as service facilities are concerned, e-Commerce falls under the umbrella of a _____ _____.

5)  _____ _____ represents the collaboration and information exchange portion of a service event.

6)  The business of business service systems goes through the following four phases: _____, _____, _____, and _____.

7)  _____ is the transfer of the ownership of a business process to a supplier, which includes management and day-to-day execution of that function.

8)  _____ is a general term that describes the relocation of a business process from one country to another.

## SELECTED READING

Friedman, T.L. (2006), *The World is Flat: A Brief History of the Twenty-First Century*, New York: Farrar, Straus and Giraux.

Sowa, John F. (2000), *Knowledge Representation: Logical, Philosophical and Computational Foundations*, Brooks Cole Publishing, Pacific Grove Publishing, Inc.

*Offshoring* (2007). http://en.wikipedia.org/wiki/Offshoring.

*Ontology* (2007). http://en.wikipedia.org/wiki/Ontology.

*Outsourcing* (2007). http://en.wikipedia.org/wiki/Outsourcing.

Maglio, P.P. (2007), *Service Science, Management, and* Engineering (SSME)*: An Interdisciplinary Approach to Service Innovation*, IBM Almaden Research Center, http://almaden.ibm.com/ssme, p. 14.

IBM Almaden Services Research (2006), *Service Science, Management, and Engineering (SSME): Challenges, Frameworks, and Call for Participation*, http://almaden.ibm.com/ssme, p. 13.

Maglio, P.P. and J. Spohrer (2007), *Fundamentals of Service Science*, IBM Almaden Research Center.

Maglio, P.P. and T. Matlock (1998), *Metaphors We Surf the Web By*, The Information Architecture Institute.

# 4

# Information Services

Through information and communications technology (ICT), modern society has made enormous advances in how we live and work. How far we have progressed is summarized by Microsoft chairman Bill Gates in a recent email message. "The ability to access and share information instantly and communicate in ways that transcend the boundaries of time and distance has given rise to an era of unprecedented productivity and innovation that has created new economic opportunities for hundreds of millions of people around the world and paved the way for global growth that is unparalleled in human history."[24]

## INFORMATION SERVICE CONCEPTS

An *information service* is a resource capable of supporting a service event or instantiating a service event based on information. In other words, an information service can assist in the execution of a service, such as in retailing, or it can actually be the service as when buying a pair of shoes on the Internet – actually, the World Wide Web, but that distinction is not required at this

---

[24] Gates, B. (2007), *The Age of Software-Powered Communications*, Electronic Mail Message, October 16, 2007 1:03:06 PM EDT.

point. The resource is a service provider that can take the form of a person or a computer. The execution of an information service event requires a service client that can also take the form of a person or computer and the provider and client must interact in order to co-produce the service. The execution of a service event changes the state of the provider and the client, but a tangible object is not produced. An information service is commonly associated with computer technology, but that is not a necessary condition. The most definitive characteristic of an information service is that the information travels, which gives rise to new models of information management and communications technology.

## A Personal Dimension

Most of the information that is communicated between people is about something. When you buy a car, the sales person tells you about the key features and how to use them. In the physician/patient relationship, the doctor and patient exchange information about a medical situation. Clearly, there is some form of informational interchange that accompanies practically all services. Information service is more than the incidental exchange of information.

With information services, the client specifically requests information and the provider supplies it using some form of communications channel. The service request may be implicit in some other form of activity or it may be "ordered" on a demand basis, but it is nevertheless requested.

## Data versus Information

Each provider/client interaction in an information service requires a context, and here is why. Pure unadulterated facts are known as *data*. For example, the date April 15$^{th}$ can mean different things to different people. To many Americans, it means tax day. To others, it may be the start of baseball. To grandmother, it may be her birth date. *Information* is data in a particular context so it has a specific meaning.

When you request some information about a subject from an Internet web site, for example, the context is supplied in some manner, such as from the site itself, the nature of the query, or even information in a previously requested web page. The context effectively gives meaning to data and turns it into information. The bits that flow through wires or through the air as electromagnetic radiation are nothing more than data, at best. Accordingly, it would be proper to say that it is an information service that turns a bunch of bits into something useful, such as a news story or downloaded music.

## Ordinary Mail

Not all information services necessarily require a computer. The United States Postal Service is a case in point, as is its international equivalent known as the PTT (Post, Telephone, and Telegraph), which do not require a computer in their basic form. Electronic mail (email as we generally know it) is also an information service, and it does require a computer. Each element has a sender and an intended recipient.

Who is the service provider? It is certainly not the sender or recipient. Clearly, it is the mail service itself. If you're thinking that the mail service is the communications channel, then you are on the right track. In this instance, and this instance only, the sender and receiver are the clients and the mail service is the service provider. In most other information services, the communications channel *is* only the channel for communication and nothing more. With mail service, pickup, transportation, and delivery would appear to be the service, and the informational content of the message is not brought into the analysis. Isn't it supposed to be private?

## Is Software a Service?

Yes. Software would appear to be a service, such as in document preparation and as suggested by the example of ordinary mail. Information is moved from one place to another and perhaps it is transformed a bit in the process. In document preparation, or word processing, as it is usually called, information is moved from an origin, such as a person's brain, through the nervous system, the person's fingers, and the keyboard to the computer and software and then to a document file. Nevertheless, it is transferred from one place to another. If electronic mail is considered to be a service, then it would seem that word processing is also. Consider another example. If you go to a tax preparation agency to have your return prepared, you consider it to be a service. If you buy a program for a small fee that does the same work as the tax agency, does it perform a service? Most people would agree that tax software is a service. In the same vein, presentation, spreadsheet, and database software would also be regarded as services.

There is another aspect to all of this, as exemplified by the word processing and email examples. The provider and client participate in the exchange of information, even though they may not be, and probably won't be, in close proximity. Thus, the distance metric is not necessarily significant in word processing, and in the case of email, even the time metric is also not significant.

Is *all* software a service? Perhaps, that should have been the original question. It is an open item. It is easy to conceptualize that office software for document preparation, presentation, graphics, data management, and data analysis could be regarded as services, since that software facilitates the transfer of information from one place to another. In the area of information systems, DSS (Decision Support System) software, for example, provides timely information to managers to aid in decision making. DSS software is definitely a service. What about AI (Artificial Intelligence) software, such as software that monitors gauges in a nuclear reactor? Then, if something goes wrong, the computer program shuts the reactor down before a meltdown occurs. Again, most people, especially those that work in nuclear power plants, would agree that it is a service. The debate could go on. For this chapter, at least, software is a service.

Practically speaking, a software package, by itself, does not qualify to be an information service. In order to be functioning as a service, software must be operating on a computer in order to respond to a client's request in an appropriate manner. You always need a computer and communications infrastructure to support software services.

# ENTERPRISE INFORMATION SERVICES

Information is the cornerstone of modern business, and government as well, and is the major ingredient in everyday commerce. In the study of information services, the distinction between information and the system to handle the information is often blurred. In this section, we will establish the difference between information and services.

## *"About" Information*

A lot of information is about things: about a product or service, about travel arrangements, about how to do something, about an event, about a person or group, about something that has happened in the past, and so forth. We are going to refer to this type of information as *operand information*, and we are additionally going to refer to information that is involved with the service process itself as *operant information*.[25] When the focus of an information service is the result, then as Vargo and Lusch might put it, we are using goods-dominant

---

[25] The distinction between operand and operant regarding services and associated information was developed by Vargo and Lusch (2004) and endorsed by IBM, as a basic abstraction of service science. See Spohrer (2007).

logic and the result is referred to as the operand. When the focus of an information service is on the process, then we are employing service-dominant logic and the operant resources are the information and the other steps in the service process.

## Business Information

Business information services are usually divided into two categories: operational services and management services. Operational services are employed to run the enterprise and management services are used to manage the enterprise. Some of the same basic concepts are used in both categories, but the time and distance characteristics are different. For example, a database management system and a database are normally used to store persistent data for the enterprise. With operational services, the database is dynamic and is updated for each transaction. With management services, static data is needed to make effective decisions. Accordingly, a static database would ordinarily be created from the dynamic database so that timely management reports could be generated. Of course, this is a bit of a simplification, but the basic idea is there.

The management of information is an enterprise service in its own right. Clearly, the transfer of information from operational databases to a data warehouse is a concrete example of an enterprise information service.

## Transaction Services

When you make an airline reservation or check a flight schedule using the Internet[26], you are using a transaction processing system. Most information services that support operational systems in today's world use transaction processing, suggested by the generic diagram in Figure 4.1 and are comprised of the following elements: client computer, communication channel, server computer, communications channel, flight operations computer, and flight database.

---

[26] You are actually using the World Wide Web, but this is a discussion for another section. If you are going to New York, for example, do you say, "I'm going by car" or do you say "I'm going by highway"? Do you fly by plane or by air? The level of specificity is important in information services.

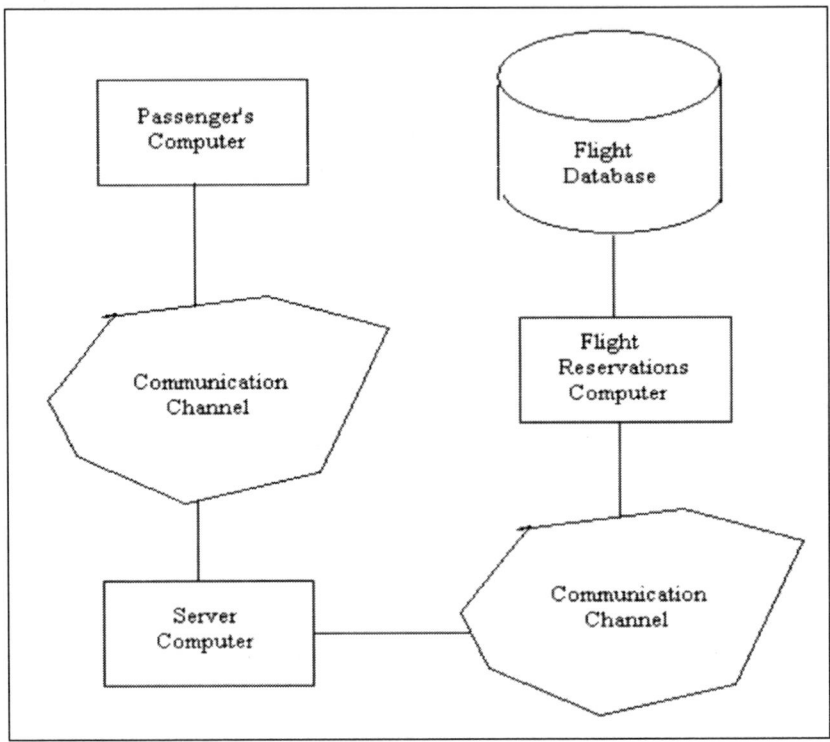

***Figure 4.1 Generic Transaction Processing Model using an Airline
Example.***

At the most general level, you interact with the server using the communications channel. You are the client, the server is the provider, and the service is the transaction. The communications channel between the passenger's computer and the server is probably the Internet. The second communications channel could be the Internet or a dedicated network. Some people call this channel the *service bus*; we will go into more detail on this subject shortly. The server computer is a client to the flight reservations computer, which is the service provider and whatever request the former makes to the latter is the service. In a similar vein, the database management system provides a service to the flight reservation computer. The entire process is mediated by hardware and software and the only thing that moves is the information.

## Information Processing

Fundamental to all the modern-day hype about the Internet, social networking, and online collaboration is the much maligned subject of data processing[27], or as it is now called "information processing." *Information processing* is what computers do to sustain business operations and comprises what we will refer to as the operant of the information service process. Information systems are the hardware, software, communications, organizational, and human facilities that sustain information processing. There are macro operations (as in macro economics) such as accessing records, sorting records, merging records, storing records, manipulating records, and reporting; and there are micro operations (again as in micro economics) such as reading, writing, moving, and performing arithmetic operations on specific pieces of data. Collectively, macro and micro operations are the substance of information services.

An effective information service requires effective information that is usually taken to mean that the information is timely, accurate, complete, relevant, accessible, verifiable, and reliable. The attributes of information determine the efficacy of an information service.

## Client and Provider Input to an Information Service

An information service requires client and provider input, just as in any other kind of service. Usually, the client – whether it is a person or a computer – enters a small amount of information into the service process. The provider – usually a computer information system – has access to a larger store of information, so that we can say the provider provisionally supplies a larger amount of information. The informational output of an information service is a function of the inputs and the nature of the service.

The client may have help supplying input to an information service through hardware and software facilities known as "interaction services." The provider may have assistance from database services and auxiliary services via a service bus.

## Interaction Services

Most people are familiar with user-friendly graphical user interfaces, known as GUIs. Desktop environments and web pages are common examples.

---

[27] In today's world of software development, there are no programmers – only software engineers. In the world of data processing, there were no programmers – only systems analysts. It is literally amazing how those 10 billion lines of COBOL code that run everyday business got written. COBOL stands for Common Business Oriented Language.

An *interaction service* is a familiar idiom for interacting with a computer. Clearly, this is a client's point of view. An interaction service is normally a socially-constructed collection of structural elements and behavioral patterns, such as action buttons, list boxes, and pull-down menus. The idea is to get information into the computer in the most efficient manner, and there are two basic methods: a command-line interface and a GUI interface. The command-line interface demands textual input and is great for a wide range of technical environments. For most clients, a GUI interface is superior, but each form of GUI requires a will-defined group of clients.

The software and hardware combination that supports client input is known as a "thin client" or a "thick client." With a *thin client*, the software for information service interaction is minimal and is usually limited to facilities provided with the computer platform that the client is using. With a *thick client*, the software for user interaction is more extensive and is tuned to a particular group of information services.

Interaction services are dependant upon what the client expects to do with the information service. Here are some examples:

Information exploration (e.g., find out about service science)

Accomplish something (e.g., reserve a seat)

Find a "good enough" answer to a question (e.g., how do we get to New York)

Change the direction of a search operation (e.g., what about service systems)

Establish a point of reference (e.g., mark my place to come back to at a later time)

Designing effective interaction services is not so easy[28] but one approach is to think about the elements that you have to work with. A common set of such elements is composed of objects (such as icons), actions (such as a file menu), subject (such as the information that you have to work with), and tools (such as calendars and appointments).

Interaction services are a small part of service science, but nevertheless an important part.

## Service Bus

A *service bus* is a high-speed data link between two computing platforms that operate in a request/response mode. The client requests an item of information (such as the price of IBM stock on Monday at 11:00 on

---

[28] See Tidwell (2006) for a comprehensive reference to designing interfaces from a practical viewpoint.

a given date) and the provider, which operates in a server mode, supplies it in an expeditious manner. A service bus requires software that is called *middleware*.

An example of the need for a service bus is inherent in the following example. A stock broker is on a line to a client who requests the price of IBM stock. The brokerage firm has a computer (the server) that gets an up-to-the-second feed from the stock exchange. There is a high speed link between the stock brokers and the server, and each broker has a specialized thick client interface. The broker enters the stock symbol for IBM into a text box and clicks a send button. The server responds in a fraction of a second with the requested price.

### Collaboration

Teams are the accepted norm in the modern enterprise, and collaboration is the process by which they progress toward a common goal. With information services, collaboration between groups and individuals can be effected from geographically dispersed locations. In general, collaboration has a well-defined structure and set of operational procedures that employs any or all of four recursive information service modalities: email, instant messaging, interactive media, and specially designed collaborative software.

Collaboration operates at the intellectual level and often benefits from decentralization and varying degrees of academic and personal diversity. Collaboration is a unique form of service. The service provider in the information service modality is established through information and communications technology, and is an instance of where the "service is the service provider," because it allows the clients in a collaboration service to exchange meaningful information.

Collaboration requires at least two clients interacting in what is referred to as a *multiclient service*. A multiclient service is frequently leaderless and is known as a *virtual organization structure*. Traditional workflow where a document is passed between team members is a common form of collaboration.

## INFORMATION SERVICE APPLICATIONS

The range of information services is multidimensional, as suggested by Figure 4.2. Information services are ubiquitous and touch on all aspects of everyday life. It would seem that everything affects everything, and the medium of exchange is information. Looking at the big picture, the three big players are people, business, and government. People interact with themselves and with business and government to engage in commerce, obtain information and services, and to participate in various forms of interpersonal communication. Businesses interact with people, other businesses, and the government to make a profit. The government interacts with other governmental entities, as well as people and businesses to provide a requisite level of service. The fuel that feeds the fire is information, which is sustained by the environment, technology, economics, and society. In the world of the Internet and the World Wide Web, information services are paramount.

## Pull versus Push

It is perhaps a bit of an oversimplification, but "the manner in which you approach an information service determines what you get." The characteristics of the *pull model* are succinctly summarized in the following sentence. "Rather than 'push,' this new approach focuses on 'pull' – creating platforms that help people to mobilize appropriate resources when the need arises." [29]

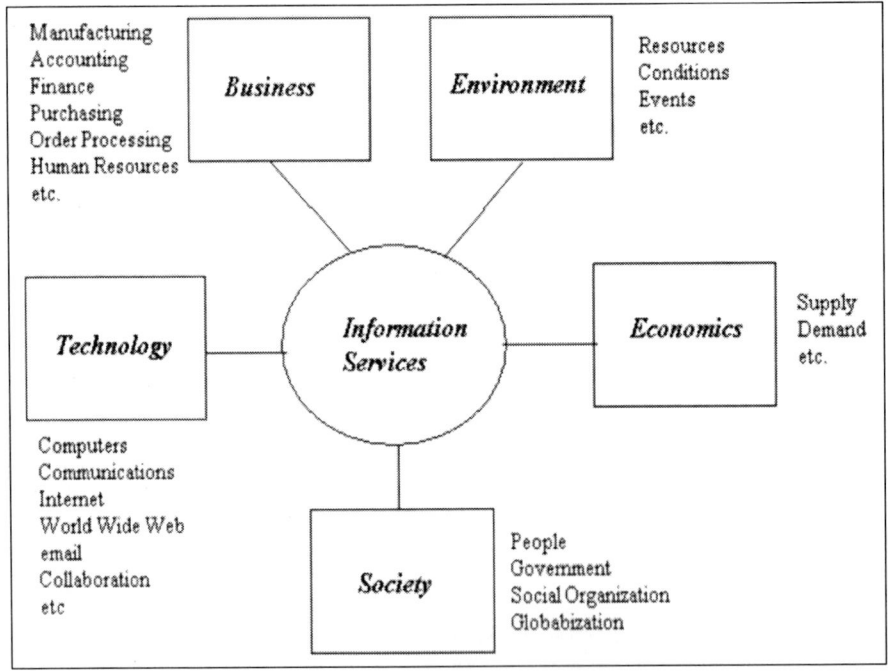

*Figure 4.2  Range of Information Services.*

[29] Hagel and Brown (2007) have identified the pull model as a means of establishing business resources for the upcoming generation of business activities based on mass communications and the Internet.

Push models are essentially scripted and thrive in stable environments with little uncertainty. Forecasting, as in demand forecasting, is key in push environments and allows high levels of efficiency to be developed in business processes. Most of modern business and governmental activity uses the push modality. A business pushes a product into the marketplace and people buy it. Push programs are top-down processes with the following steps: design, deploy, execute, monitor, and refine.

Pull models increase value creation for both clients and providers. For clients, "pull" activity expands the scope of available resources. For providers, pull systems expand the market for services. Pull platforms are associated with the following attributes: uncertain demand, emergent design, decentralized environment, loosely coupled modular construction of facilities, and on-demand service provisioning. Pull models are more amenable to uncertain business conditions.

From both the client's and the provider's perspectives, pull services focus on the following activities: find, select, purchase, deliver, and service. If all of this sounds familiar, it should be. It represents how you buy shoes on the Internet.

## Enterprise Service Constituents

The seven constituents of an enterprise information service are providers, clients, messages, communications, information processing, persistent storage, and the user interface that collectively take into consideration the requisite technology including database facilities, email archives, protocols, business rules, operational procedures, and a variety of service interactions needed for enterprise applications. Since information and not people move in information services, this category of service is based on information and communications technology. It is important that when we discuss information services at the enterprise level, we are primarily concerned with functionality and not necessarily with computing platforms.

## Information Service Model

Information service systems typically operate in a client/server mode, which means that the end user is the service client, the enterprise application running on a computing platform is the service provider, and the means of client and provider interaction is some form of communications channel. Typically, the client enters information into the system through a well-defined interface and the provider does something in return. Exactly what the provider does is of primary importance to the information service system.

There are at least three distinct possibilities:

1.  The provider accesses some form of persistent storage and returns selected information to the client.

2.  The provider performs some element of information processing and returns an indicator to the client that it was done.

3.  The client and the provider enter into an interactive dialog concerning specific informational elements and a supply chain operation is initiated to accomplish the corresponding enterprise operation.

As such, information service systems are instrumental in supporting daily activities. Typical business applications are order processing, purchasing, accounting, inventory control, human resources, marketing and sales support, manufacturing, and various forms of service support including data collection and information management.

An *enterprise resource planning* (ERP) service is an integrated collection of constituent applications operating at the enterprise level that provide information services in six comprehensive areas: production, supply chain, customer relationship management, sales support and ordering, financial and managerial accounting, and human resources. An ERP service essentially operates by using a cross section of diverse traditional business applications to satisfy client requests for information and is particularly appropriate to a global environment. Customer relationship management (CRM) is frequently presented as a separate topic.

## Scope of Electronic Information Services

It is possible to be more definitive about electronic information services. Figure 4.3 depicts the three main constituents, introduced earlier, and how the information services are related. The diagram reflects the emphasis in electronic information services. B2C means business-to-consumer. B2B means business-to-business. G2B means government-to-business. C2C means consumer-to-consumer. G2G means government-to-government. G2C means government-to-consumer. In the symbols, the leftmost letter reflects the provider and the rightmost letter represents the client.

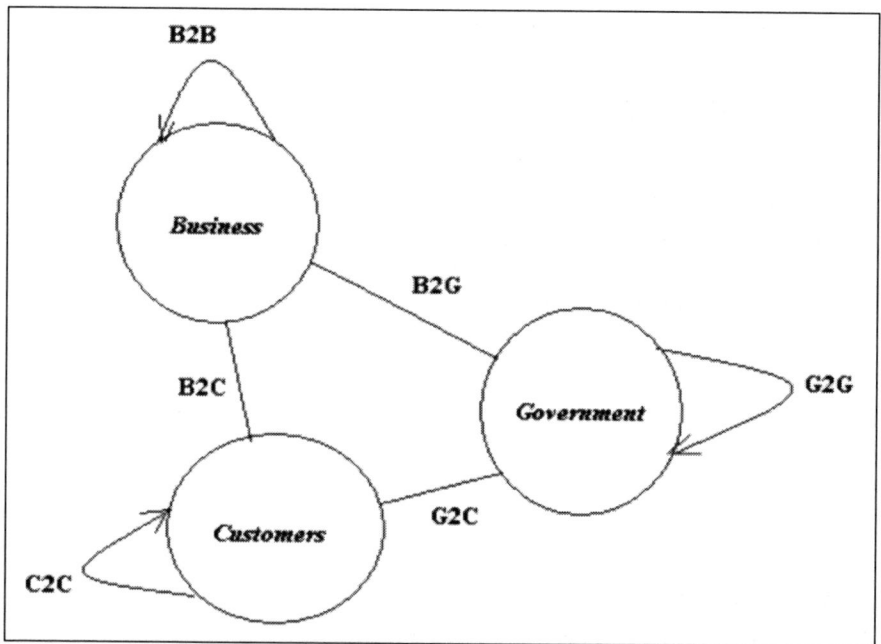

*Figure 4.3 Scope of Information Services.*

## Electronic Commerce

Electronic commerce is an enterprise information service application supported by the Internet and the World Wide Web, and can be viewed as an opportunistic means of doing business with minimal cost. In short, the information services of the Internet and the Web are used to conduct business.

Electronic commerce is usually known as e-commerce or B2C for short. Conventional business establishments are referred to as "brick and mortar" facilities characterized by a shopping area in which customers can view products, and business personnel can conduct commerce. The equivalent in the digital world is an e-commerce web site where a consumer can conduct analogous functions. The service provider is the e-commerce web site and the customer is the client connected to the web site via the Internet, as suggested by Figure 4.4. In this instance, the Internet is the communications channel. The service process is the set of interactions between the customer and one or more web sites that go through the following steps: find, select, purchase, deliver, and service.

*Find* is an Internet service process, which is usually a set of service interactions, to navigate to the desired Internet retailer. After the electronic retailer is chosen, the *select* and *purchase* services represent the online equivalent of the traditional processes of making a purchase. Purchasing involves payment that invokes a secure service designed for that specific purpose. *Deliver* is another service process initiated by the retailer for physically delivering the product to the consumer. *Service* is the Web enabled service process of providing customer support. Each of the steps in the B2C service process (i.e., find, select, purchase, deliver, and service) involves at least one service, so the entire process can be properly regarded as a *multiservice*, driven by a series of constituent information services.

B2C transactions are characterized by increased convenience, enhanced efficiency, additional buying choice, and lower prices, from the consumer's perspective, and by an increased return on retailing investment for the electronic retailer. An electronic retailer need not have a related "brick and mortar" facility, but that is often the case.

## Electronic Business

Electronic business is the use of the Internet and the World Wide Web to conduct business operations, including intra-business and inter-business transactions. This is a broad category and ranges from relatively simple information services to obtain tacit business information from within a single organization to complex Web Services and REST web services.[30]

---

[30] Web Services and REST are covered under "Services Technology." REST stands for Representational State Transfer and is a means of conducting electronic business without an extensive Web Services infrastructure.

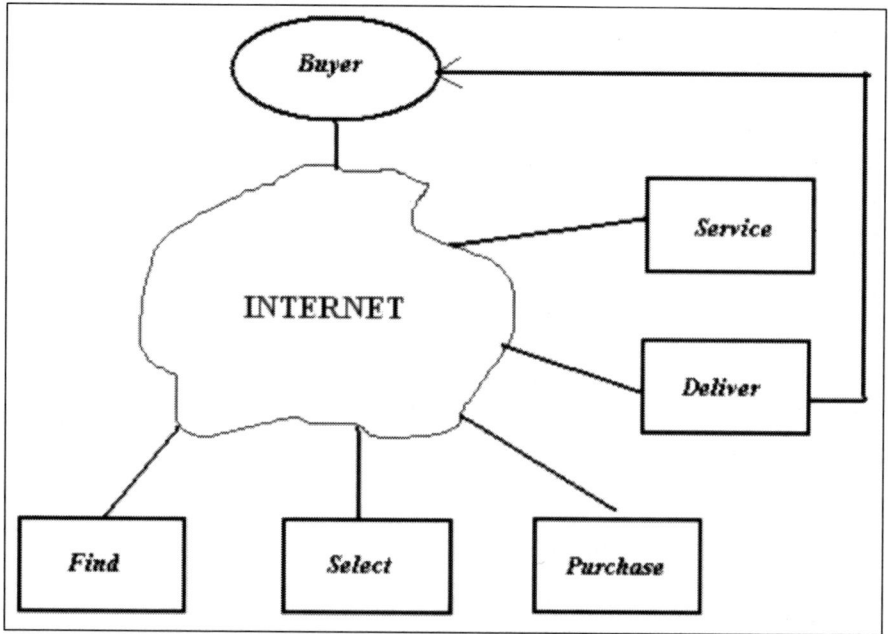

*Figure 4.4  Conceptualization of Electronic Commerce.*

Electronic business is usually known as e-business or B2B for short and has its roots in electronic data interchange (EDI) commonly used to exchange information on business operations within an organization, and between business partners, suppliers, and wholesalers.  The use of the Internet for communications services reduces operational costs for computer networks and increases the value obtained from costs that are incurred.

The major advantage of B2B operations is that companies can utilize an information service known as the "B2B Electronic Marketplace," wherein they can buy and sell products and exchange information through a *virtual marketplace* .  Not only can companies create supply chains, but they can create business partnerships in which one company can take advantage of information   services of another company.  The process, known as the *componentization of information services*, facilitates the creation of web services that allow the company to be a more responsive (to market and economic conditions) enterprise.

B2B is similar to B2C in one respect.  Modern company operations require the purchase of certain *indirect materials*, typically referred to as MRO materials, where MRO stands for "maintenance, repair, and operations," and include such items as ball pens, repair parts, and office equipment.  Through the B2B electronic marketplace, as reflected in Figure 4.5, various companies can collectively achieve lower cost through *demand aggregation.*

*Direct materials* are items used in production or retail operations as part of a company's core business. Through web services (see Chapters 5 and 6), B2B operations can also be sustained in this area.

## Electronic Marketplace

Information services, such as the electronic marketplace, permit companies to engage in B2B market operations in horizontal and vertical electronic marketplaces. In a *horizontal marketplace*, buyers and sellers can interact across many industries. Travel and financial services are common examples, because they are applicable to almost any type of business, such as the process industries (oil and gas) and conventional and electronic retailing.

In a *vertical marketplace*, buyers and sellers are in the same industry and primarily engage in information services that relate to direct material.

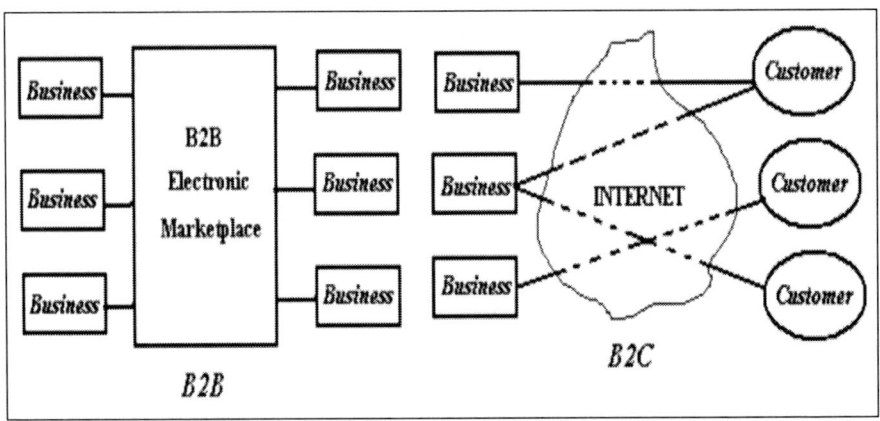

*Figure 4.5  B2B Versus B2C Marketplaces.*

## Electronic Government

Information services are a means of transforming the management and operations of government to be more responsive, efficient, and reliable in delivering services to the electorate – at all governmental levels, including federal, state, and local communities. The objective is to enhance informational facilities that already exist so they may properly be regarded as "click and mortar," with the options of obtaining information and services via the Internet and World Wide Web while continuing to have a physical presence. Three flavors have been identified: Government to Business (G2B), Government to Consumer (G2C), and Government to Government (G2G). In the latter case, there are two possibilities: inter-government and intra-government. Inter-government refers to the vertical alignment of information services between governmental levels on the same initiative, such as the coordination of federal, state, and local agencies on air pollution. Intra-government refers to the horizontal alignment of services between agencies at the same level of government, such as disaster response coordination between police, fire, and emergency medical departments.

Government to business operations reflect information services that cover purchasing of MRO materials, and the provisioning of information facilities for procedures, regulations, reporting, and compliance. In the latter case, governmental reporting facilities (by business to government) are commonly available to submit requisite documentation through Internet and World Wide Web services.

Most citizens are familiar with Government to consumer information services for taxes and various forms of registration. For taxpayers, the ability to download forms and directions and the ability to submit completed tax forms are paramount. For those of us fortunate enough to receive a tax refund, the increased efficiency is money in the bank. Vehicle and voter registration are other information services that are efficient from both client and provider perspectives.

Overall, however, the availability of information on dates, procedures, directions, and so forth, at the click of a mouse via the Internet and the World Wide Web – pure information services – is the greatest advantage of G2C services.

# PERSONAL INFORMATION SERVICES

Personal information services are an ever expanding collection of Internet and World Wide Web applications. The prevalence of the applications, however, brings up a fundamental question about exactly what constitutes the clients, providers, and the services in the various forms of information service. The resources appear to be different among the applications, so the presentation of the subject matter will be instructive for determining the scope of personal information services. Accordingly, we will cover the following services: chat rooms, instant messaging, Internet telephone, web auctions, user-generated media, social networking, and newsgroups. This is only a sample of relevant applications but is indicative of how information services are used to support those applications.

## Chat Rooms

One of the most popular means of communicating on the Internet is through a char room, the best known of which is IRC (Internet Relay Chat). IRC operates in the client/server mode and requires an IRC server; clients require special IRC software, usually downloaded from the Internet.

When using chat, the user selects a channel, which establishes the conversation in which the user will participate. Characteristically, other users, throughout the world, will have chosen the same channel. The idea being that they will exchange information on a certain subject.

During operation, users type messages on their local client computer and the information is relayed via the Internet to the server. The message is then forwarded to other users signed on to the same channel and is displayed on their screens. A user may just listen, figuratively speaking, or may participate in the conversation. Ostensibly, users respond to other users' transmissions, so that an identifying name (sometimes called a *handle*) accompanies each submission. Since chat rooms are a global phenomena, a network of IRC servers is required to service all of the users in a specific domain. A recent development is "voice chat," which is an audio equivalent to the traditional text-based chat.

At the end-user level, a chat room can be viewed as a collection of clients whose interpersonal communications is being managed by the chat server system operating as a service provider. The chat server system consists of the hardware, software, and Internet facilities, necessary to do the task. The service process consists of a set of dynamically determined client/server interactions, where the end-user is the client and the chat server is the service provider.

## Instant Messaging

Instant messaging is the private real-time communication of textual messages between two users logged on to an instant messaging (IM) server over the Internet. Messages are forwarded through an IM server that uses the "sender" client's buddy list to determine the destination for forwarded messages.

Many Internet specialists consider instant messaging to be a form of chat room operations, since it has similar information service characteristics.

## Front and Back Stages

Internet chat and instant messaging, among other information services, incorporate a value chain of component services, divided between front and back stages.[31] Essentially, the front stage is what the end-user conceptualizes and the back stage is what is going on under the covers, so to speak.

The noteworthy aspect of the division is that human clients are only part of the process, if they are involved at all, and the front stage represents the client's experience supplemented by the back stage that represents the information service support structure based on ICT facilities. The participants (Human or ICT) may possess different but complementary views of the service process.

## Internet Telephone

Using the Internet for making telephone calls is appealing to many people because of the cost, which may be free in some cases, over and above the cost of the Internet connection. Several methods and associated software facilities are available. They generally fall into two broad categories.

In the first case, you use special hardware and software to communicate through your personal computer (PC) using a microphone and speakers. If you are calling someone who is also using the same method, the call is totally free, as it is with web browsing and email, and it is also applicable to users anywhere in the world.

In the second case, you use your ordinary "land line" telephone handset, and the call is routed over the Internet using a service process generally known as Voice over IP (VoIP).[32] With VoIP, your voice is digitized and routed through the Internet as information packets, similar to other information services such as web pages and email. At the receiving end, the voice packets are converted to normal telephone signals.

With Internet telephone, the conceptualized front and back stages coincide. The clients are the telephone users and the service provider is the value chain of Internet activities.

---

[31] See Tabas (2007).

[32] IP is the protocol for routing messages through the various inter-connected networks as packets of information. IP stands for Internet Protocol.

## Web Auctions

A *web auction* is an Internet and World Wide Web service that connects buyers and sellers in a consumer-to-consumer (C2C) mode to conduct an online version of traditional auction. A well-known web site that manages the web auction process is *eBay*, but there are notably other sites that perform the same service.

In this instance, the information service is the posting and delivery of information concerning products for sale and associated bids. The clients are the buyers and sellers and the information service consists of the information processing facilities to sustain the auction. In this instance, the Internet and the World Wide Web serve only as a communication channel.

## User Generated Media

There are three major forms of information dissemination normally originating from individuals that use the Internet and World Wide Web services: web logs, podcasts, and RSS feeds[33]. The services are related and are covered together in this section.

A *web log* (called a *blog*) is a medium for presenting information without restrictions or review over the Internet and accessible through the World Wide Web. People who participate in the service of creating information content in this category are known as *bloggers*, and the process itself is known as *blogging*[34]. The following three information services are normally associated with this form of activity: (1) Obtaining information on how to set up and access a blog web site; (2) Providing services that assist in actually setting up a blog web site; and (3) Using services that assist in making entries in a web log. Each blog site has a uniform resource locator (URL)[35] and a theme, subsequently used for search and discovery.

Clearly, the information services needed for accessing blogs are traditional web searches, wherein you request information and it is returned to you using pull technology.[36] Individuals use search engines, such as Google, to locate blog sites. For example, if you were interested in people's opinions on "broccoli," you would do a search with the following search phrase:

---

[33] RSS stand for Read Simple Syndication.
[34] There is no name for people who just read web logs.
[35] A URL, such as www.ibm.com, is a means of accessing a web site.
[36] Recall that with pull technology, you have to access information (i.e., request it), whereas with push technology, it is sent to you automatically. Normally, you have to set up "push" sites beforehand.

```
broccoli blog
```

and *voila*, you could find out what some people think about the vegetable. There are search engines designed specifically for searching blog sites.

A *podcast* is an audio blog, serviced by the Internet, that serves the same purpose as a personal radio station. Using your PC and a microphone, you can record a document and store it on an appropriate blog site. Other users can then download the audio blog to their PC for listening or for transfer to a music player. Podcasts are used to listen to broadcast media nd educational material. In the latter category, a podcast is an effective means of delivering course material to students.

An *RSS feed* is a means of generating a wider audience for blogs and podcasts, through an Internet technique known as Really Simple Syndication. RSS feeds utilize special web formatted material and deliver automatically generated downloads to registered end users using push technology.

User-generated media operations are generally considered to be a front stage process. All communications are *asynchronous*, which means they are created (or uploaded) as a process at one time and accessed (or downloaded) by another process at another time, using push technology.

## Social Networking

Social networking is usually regarded as the process of keeping up with friends and family, and it is no surprise that the process has migrated to the World Wide Web. The inherent information service is social networking is known as "shared space."

A *shared space* is an online virtual public space in which a peson – usually a young person – can display information about themselves, including text, audio, and video. Special web sites, such as MySpace and Facebook, are designed to handle social networking. Actually, the video is predominantly photographs taken with a digital camera and uploaded to an appropriate web site set up for social networking.

A person's virtual space is subsequently accessible by friends. The conceptual model for a shared space is that of a private room to which one can invite friends to look around, thus giving the owner a private virtual space not otherwise available in everyday life.

As with information services that support media, social networking services are asynchronous and use pull technology.

## Newsgroups

A *newsgroup* is a collection of people that participate in a discussion on a particular subject using Internet facilities. The usual form of communication is email, and the mode of communication is question and answer. The largest and most widely known online news group is *usenet*.

A participant subscribes to a particular topic. When that participant logs on to the newsgroup server, the entries on the selected topic are automatically sent to that participant.

Special client software is required to participate in a newsgroup. User interactions are organized by thread, so that a given user effectively engages in a conversation, as required, with participants in the same interest group. If a thread is *moderated*, questions are sent to a human moderator who screens the questions for appropriateness. Otherwise, questions are simply listed by topic. Most threads are archived by date.

Newsgroup software employs the same information service modality as email, and in fact, is dependent upon email for its operational infrastructure. Newsgroup facilities are also available through most information service portals, such as America Online and Google. With Google, you can access newsgroups via http://groups.google.com.

# SUMMARY

An *information service* is a resource capable of supporting a service event or instantiating in a service event based on information. In other words, an information service can assist in the execution of a service, such as in retailing, or it can actually be the service as when buying a pair of shoes on the Internet.

Most of the information that is communicated between people is about something. With information services, the client requests information and the provider supplies it using some form of communications channel.

Software would appear to be a service, such as in document preparation and as suggested by the example of ordinary mail. Information is moved from one place to another and perhaps it is transformed a bit in the process.

Information is the cornerstone of modern business, and government as well, and is the major ingredient in everyday commerce. Business information services are usually divided into two categories: operational services and management services. Operational services are employed to run the enterprise and management services are used to manage the enterprise.

When you make an airline reservation or check a flight schedule using the Internet[37], you are using a transaction processing system. Transaction processing systems are the cornerstone of modern business.

Teams are the accepted norm in the modern enterprise, and collaboration is the process by which they progress toward a common goal. With information services, collaboration between groups and individuals can be effected from geographically dispersed locations.

Major enterprise information service applications are electronic commerce, electronic business, and electronic government. Major personal information service applications are chat rooms, instant messaging, Internet telephone, web auctions, web logs, podcasts, RSS feeds, social networking, and newsgroups.

## KEY TERMINOLOGY

The reader should be familiar with the following terms in the context in which they were used in the chapter.

Blog
Blogger
Blogging
Business-to-business
Business-to-consumer
Chat room
Collaboration
Consumer-to-consumer
Deliver
Electronic data interchange
Find
Government-to-business
Government-to-consumer
Government-to-government
Handle
ICT
Information
Information service
Interaction service

---

[37] You are actually using the World Wide Web, but this is a discussion for another section. If you are going to New York, for example, do you say, "I'm going by car" or do you say "I'm going by highway"? Do you fly by plane or by air? The level of specificity is important in information services.

Middleware
Multiclient service
Multiservice
Operand information
Operant information
Podcast
Pull model
Purchase
Push model
RSS
Select
Service
Service bus
Social networking
Thick client
Thin client
URL
Virtual marketplace
Virtual organization structure
VoIP
Web log

# A FEW GOOD QUESTIONS[38]

1) An _____ _____ is a service capable of supporting a service event or instantiating a service event based on information.

2) ICT is an acronym for _____ ___ _____ _____ _____.

3) Information that is involved with the service process itself is known as _____ _____.

4) A _____ ___ is a high-speed data link between two computing platforms that operate in a request/response mode.

_____

[38]Answers: (1) information service; (2) information and communications technology; (3) operant information; (4) service bus; (5) find, select, purchase, deliver, service; (6) the Internet; (7) podcast.

5) The service process for e-commerce consists of the following five steps: _____, _____, _____, _____, and _____.

6) VoIP uses ___ _____ as the communications channel.

7) A _____ is an audio blog serviced by the Internet.

## SELECTED READING

Gralla, P., *How the Internet Works*, Indianapolis, IN: Que Publishing, 2004.

Hagel, J. and J.S. Brown (2007), *From Push to Pull: Emerging Models for Mobilizing Resources,* www.edgeperspectives.com.

Richardson, L. and S. Ruby , RESTful Web Services, Sebastopol, DA; O'Reilly Media, Inc., 2007.

Spohrer, J., Vargo, S.C., Caswell, N., and P.P. Maglio (2007), *The Service System is the Basic Abstraction of Service Science*, IBM Research, Almaden Research Center, San Jose, CA, www.almaden.ibm.com/asr.

Stair, R.M. and G.W. Reynolds, *Principles of Information Systems: A Managerial Approach*, Boston: Thomson Course Technology, 2008.

Tabas, L., *Designing for Service Systems*, UCB iSchool Report 2007-008, February, 2007.

Tapscott, D. and A.D. Williams, *Wikinomics: How Mass Collaboration Changes Everything*, New York: Penguin Group, Ic., 2006.

Tidwell, J., *Designing Interfaces*, Sebastopol, CA: O'Reilly Media, Inc., 2006.

Vargo, S. and B. Lusch, "Evolving to a New Dominant Logic for Marketing," *Journal of Marketing*, 69 (January, 2004), 1-17.

Vargo, S. and B. Lusch, *Service-Dominant Logic Basics*, www.sdlogic.net, 2007.

# 5

# Service Management

Service management is an established subject that has recently been rejuvenated through IT enablement. Heretofore, the focus in service management has been on the application of traditional management concepts to enterprise processes that primarily involve services. Typical business examples are banking and health care that have greatly benefited from the application of scientific principles to everyday operations. Two common applications are the use of waiting-line methods for the front office and process scheduling techniques for the back office. Through the application of information and communications technology (ICT), many organizations have encapsulated everyday operations enabling them to go through a transformational process to achieve revenue growth by being able to respond more quickly to changing market conditions and by being more effective and efficient in the application of services. This chapter describes modern services management. The viewpoint taken here is that services management employs computer concepts, but its domain is by no means restricted to computer-based services and includes just about any service that a person can imagine.

# SERVICE MANAGEMENT CONCEPTS

There are three forces operating in the sphere of service processes. The first is the use of ICT as an enabler in providing revenue growth, efficiency, and effectiveness for traditional and enhanced services, as well as for conventional business processes. This subject is commonly referred to as information systems. The second is the consulting services domain that provides IT services to external organizations. The third is the use of ICT to manage information systems and services, which is a field of endeavor known as IT Services Management. Briefly said, it is the use of computers to manage the enterprise and also to manage itself.

## *Information Technology*

Information Technology (IT), as a discipline, has been around for awhile and has heretofore been regarded as computer hardware and software in support of both personal and enterprise activities. With widespread acceptance of the Internet, the World Wide Web, and advanced information systems, as well as enhanced personal productivity aids, the abbreviation has taken on a more inclusive meaning to include all of the activities mentioned, in addition to many organizational and workforce assets. Figure 5.1 gives a conceptual view of the new IT. When most modern executives refer to IT, as in "We will have to increase the IT budget for next year," they are referring to people, technology, and organization.

***Figure 5.1 Conceptual View of the New Information Technology.***

## Domain of Service Management

Many people feel that what you see in the world depends on the lens through which you are looking.[39]  So if you adopt a service-centric point of view, most socially-developed phenomena can be viewed as services.[40]  It follows that if we are going to manage services, we should at least consider to whom services are applied and how the service delivery is achieved.

Eventually, this gets us to the service provider type and the service object, but instead of dwelling on people and possessions, we are going to focus on an organizational setting consisting of people and everyday operational units. The *service provider*, in this instance, is a person acting in a service capacity or a group of persons, including support facilities, that has adopted a role of a service provider.  The *service object* is another person or operational unit, usually referred to as a *business unit*.  In the latter case, the service object need not be part of the same organization as the service provider.  Some examples of service relationships are: (1) an accounting department in a manufacturing company; (2) a computer support person in an academic department; (3) a consulting group that services external customers; (4) an IT department that serves several business units in the same organization; and of course (5) a service professional serving several clients.

There are at least three different types of provider arrangements:[41]

**Type I:**   The service provider delivers services to only one service object.

**Type II:**  The service provider delivers services to more than one service object in the same organization.

**Type III:** The service provider delivers services to one or more service objects in external organizations.

Once a provider type is identified, in a particular instance, the next step is to determine who pays for the service and specifically how that support is organized. This process is known as *service provisioning*.

---

[39] You can call this a *service lens*.  On the other hand, it has been observed that if you have only one tool, such as a hammer, then everything in the world is a nail.

[40] Some service scientists even go so far as to say that when you buy a product, such as a car, you are actually buying the service that the car provides, and not the physical object.  The point of view, taken here, is that products are still products, and the tenets for services, given in chapter one, such as co-production, intangibility, and heterogeneity, still apply.

[41] A good reference to this topic is *An Introductory Overview of ITIL® V3*, The IT Service Management Forum, itSMF, 2007.

There are two sides to every coin, so there is a complementary set of client arrangements.

**Type IV:** The client receives services from only one service provider.

**Type V:** The client receives services from more than one service provider in the same organization as the client.

**Type VI:** The client receives services from one or more service providers in external organizations.

**Type VII:** Any combination of types IV through VI.

Next in the domain of service management, is the delineation of the key activities performed to support service provisioning, such as incident management, problem management, and change management. Overall, the internal processes of effective service management go through a cyclic process, known as the *service lifecycle* that includes service strategy, service design, service transition, service operation, and continual service improvement.

The use of the methodology presented in this chapter is known as *best practices*. Most service organizations and all IT organizations would perform better if they adopted a set of best practices, and clearly, many of them do.

## Service as a Business

The notion of service has its origin in ancient times and was understood to mean "one person doing something for another." With the advent of civilization and industrialization, the definition of service was implicitly extended to encompass "one person doing something for an organization," usually in the form of employment. At this stage, specialization and entrepreneurship kicked in with all of their rights and privileges resulting in what we now recognize as the service organization.

Specialization has its roots in process efficiency, but has definite social overtones. Some jobs are more lucrative and have more prestige, and for a variety of reasons, people can do some tasks better than others. Specialization is not limited to individuals but applies to organizations and groups within organizations, as well. Specialization is commonplace, not only in service organizations. In conventional business processes, such as a sales group, certain tasks are performed more expeditiously by a single individual or group, as with credit checking, when the task is performed repeatedly. The degree of specialization needed in a service process is related to the amount of repeatability. Most production and service chains divide the process into individual tasks that are performed by a single unit, taken here to be a person, group, or machine, such that efficiency and effectiveness is achieved through specialization.

Innovation flourishes in a receptive service environment, so that effective service groups are commonly at odds with their parent organization. Service spin offs have resulted in a thriving service economy through entrepreneurship and innovation.

Accordingly, it is important to recognize that *service is a business*, and that the principles given here apply equally well to internal and external service organizations.

## Service Componentization

Services are ubiquitous so practically everyone knows what one is. Well, maybe they can't exactly define it, but they recognize one when they see or experience it. What most people don't think about, unless they have to, is that a service is a process. Beneath the surface, there is usually a collection of activities to support that process. The activities are organized into components.

A *component* is an organizational entity for instantiating services. Some components provide more than one service and some services are comprised of more that one component. The operation of a simple restaurant is used to clarify the concept of componentization.[42]

We go to a restaurant for a meal. The meal is the service we are seeking. We grab a table, look at the menu, and give our order to a waiter or waitress. Subsequently, the meal is delivered. We consume the meal, pay the tab, and leave. In our interaction with the waiter or waitress, we exchange information, so in a very general sense, we co-produce the service event, although we do not experience the meal preparation. This is not a pure service, since the food is a product. However, the service part of the meal is a service.

On the other hand, we all know that the restaurant is a collection of interacting components that provide a meal service to one or more guests. The components of the restaurant are the server (i.e., the waiter or waitress), the kitchen (that prepares the food), a cleaning component, a food-ordering component, an accounting component, a facility-management component, and a restaurant management component that orchestrates the services supplied by the components. The *service orchestration*, which is an explicit or implicit specification of the

---

[42] Adapted from Hurwitz, Bloor, Baroudi, and Kaufman (2007), which is arguably the most readable and comprehensive book on service-oriented architecture.

interactions between components, is a necessary element in the design of a managed service system.

Collectively, the arrangements of components that make up a service offering constitute its architecture. In service architecture, some components are internal persons or units, some components are outsourced, and some components are business partners. One aspect of service management is the choreography of components in a particular business process – that is, how information or tasks is passed between components without explicit direction.

Another important aspect of service management is keeping track of the components and their attributes. When service organizations get complicated, a service repository is required to keep track of the services that are provided by each component and what components are needed for a particular service process. Usually, a computer database is used. From a strategic viewpoint, a component is an asset that must be managed just as any other asset.

# SERVICE MANAGEMENT LIFECYCLE

Information is a critical asset in the operation of an enterprise and in the everyday lives of individuals. In a figurative sense, information is the grease that allows the components to work together. IT is employed to handle the information needed to manage the operations of an enterprise and to aid in making effective decisions. Thus, IT is a service to the enterprise, regardless if that enterprise is concerned with production processes, service operations, government reporting, professional services, scientific services, technical services, or personal services. Frequently, this area is referred to as information systems, and examples are doctor scheduling and record keeping, web page design, billing, enterprise resource planning (ERP), customer relationship management (CRM), supply chain management (SCM), and various forms of e-commerce. IT services are the underpinnings of critical information systems. The facility, known as *IT services*, is something that an enterprise might provide to itself and also to outside customers, if it is engaged in that area of endeavor.

## IT Services Sourcing

There are several aspects of IT services that can vary between organizations. Examples are commonplace: computer operations, network management, hardware and software acquisition, system analysis and design, software design, software development, information systems integration, and call center and help desk operation and management. This is a representative set of tasks necessary for sustaining an IT services organization. You can do them yourself; you can have another business entity help you do them; or you can have a business entity do them for you. In the latter two cases, the business process is known as *IT service outsourcing*.

Most IT services reflect an underlying set of IT assets, such as hardware, software, users, and systems. The IT services organization has three possible roles regarding these assets: develop or acquire, operate, and manage. For each of the IT assets, role adoption can differ. For example, hardware can be acquired internally and operated by an outside contractor.

The entity that provides the service, that is, the external business unit, need not be an independent business entity in a foreign country. It can be a separate business unit in the same enterprise, located locally, in the same country, or offshore. Alternately, it can be an independent professional services business entity in the same country – a service usually regarded as *IT consulting*. In many cases, however, the organization providing the outsourced service *is*, in fact, an independent business entity operating out of and located in a foreign country.

## IT Services Management

It would seem that a person's view of IT services management would be different, depending on whether your organization is the service provider or the service client, and indeed, it is. The common denominator between the various perspectives is the set of common issues that business and IT managers have to deal with, some of which are strategic planning, IT and business alignment, measurement and analysis, costs and investment, business partners and relationships, sourcing, continuous improvement, and governance. The issues are repetitive, recurring, and ongoing, and constitute a *service lifecycle*. The elements of the lifecycle are generic and do not necessarily apply to all service systems. Differences lie in the adoption and deployment of the lifecycle elements.

At the heart of IT services management is a set of tasks that involve "keeping track of things," and there are a lot of things to keep track of. We will call them *service elements*. Some of the service elements are obvious, such as users, hardware, software, network components, office facilities, and configurations. There are other service elements, mostly related to enterprise operations that can offer a challenge, such as categorization of services, to whom those services are supplied or alternately, from whom those services are obtained, contractors, outsourced projects, outsourcers, and business partners. A *service directory* is needed for this type of record keeping. Lastly, with regard to business alignment and service operations, there is a whole host of service operational elements that collectively possess business value that should not be ignored. Three of many such service operational elements are incident management, problem management, and change management. It is through the integration of service operational elements that an enterprise can achieve significant business value. The subject is covered in a later section in this chapter.

## Elements of the Service Lifecycle

The service lifecycle consists of five important elements, listed as follows: Service Strategy, Service Design, Service Transition, Service Operation, and Continuous Improvement. Figure 5.2 is a waterfall model that suggests how the requirements process goes from strategy to continuous improvement, implementing a feedback process as required. Each element of the service lifecycle is considered separately.

## Service Strategy

The first and most important element in the service lifecycle is service strategy. Successful service operations are not sustainable over long periods, because of environmental turbulence affecting resources, competition, and requirements. Accordingly, a service strategy is needed. A *strategy* is a long term plan, based on objectives, that allows an organization to adapt to changing conditions.

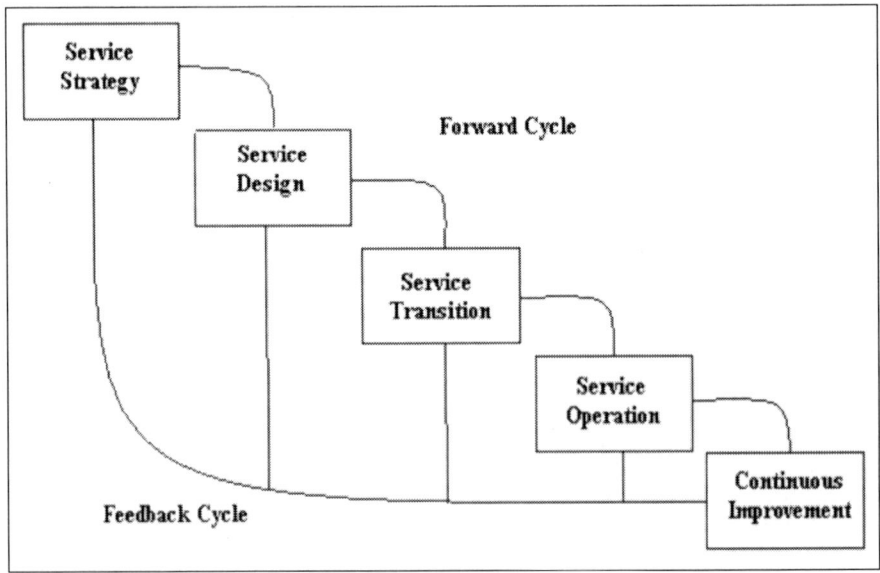

*Figure 5.2 Service Lifecycle.*

Since service is a client[43] based endeavor, it is necessary that a service delivers perceptible value, so that a service strategy based on client needs is necessary for successful service operations. A service strategy, recorded in s *strategy document*, should reflect whether the strategy is intended for a provider or a client.

A service strategy would consist of two kinds of elements: disparate elements that differ between provider and client, and common elements that are essentially common to both provider and client. The disparate service elements deal with the service itself, the marketplace, and the service value determination. The common elements deal with service level, service provisioning, and service portfolio management.

For the provider, the service elements are:

What services should be offered
Who the clients are

For the client, the service elements are:

*What services should be obtained*
*Where or from whom should the services be obtained*

For the provider, the marketplace elements are:

Selling environment (internal, local, national, international)
Selling competition

For the client, the marketplace elements are:

Sourcing environment (internal, local, national, international)
Sourcing options

For the provider, the value determination elements are:

Projected revenue
Resources needed (people, organization, technology)

For the client, the value determination elements are:

Projected costs
Resources required (people, organization, technology)

For the provider and client, the service level elements are:

Measurement and analysis

---

[43] In some cases, use of the term "customer" would be more amenable with IT services. We will continue with the term "client" because of the provider/client model adopted in earlier chapters.

Service management functions
Critical success factors

For the provider and client, the service provisioning elements are:

Managed service
Shared service
Utility service

Lastly, for the provider and client, the service portfolio element is a database of the total service package.

As far as how an organization uses a service strategy is concerned, it is an individual matter. A service document should reflect major items, such as whether services are managed internally or outsourced, who the key collaborators are, and what service management functions, such as problem and incident management functions, are needed.

## Service Design

Service design refers to the synthesis of services to satisfy enterprise objectives. This stage has general applicability, even though it appears, on the surface to reflect IT services. Service design incorporates service architecture, processes, policies, and requisite documentation. Even though the service strategy phase identifies services, the service design phase is where they are established to satisfy business objectives. Even though a computer-based service is developed offshore, it is usually developed by the parent organization during this phase. Risks, quality, measurement, and infrastructure requirements are specified in this stage. Also, this stage involves capacity management, availability management, security management, and key organizational responsibilities.

## Service Transition

Service transition concerns the implementation of services in the sense of putting them into a production environment. As such, service transition is an organizational bridge between the design and the operations stages. In many instances, the service transition phase involves a change to existing services involving limited functionality and operational procedures. As such, a service transition requires the establishing of or adhering to a formal policy for the implementation of required changes and the development of a framework for the integration of the changes. When additional training and help desk support is needed, it is established in the service transition stage, which may also include system validation and testing.

## Service Operation

The function of the service operation stage is to manage and deliver the services established in the design stage. Business value to the enterprise is delivered in the operation phase, and event monitoring is of prime importance. A *service event* is a change of state during the delivery of a service that requires attention, such as an unplanned interruption of service. Two service management functions are commonly involved: incident management and problem management. *Incident management* is primarily concerned with resolving the situation and getting the system back up and running. *Problem management* focuses on determining the root cause of an event and interfaces with change management to insure that the problem is not a recurrent event.

## Continuous Improvement

Continuous improvement, or more properly, *Continuous Service Improvement*, refers to the process of maintaining value to the enterprise of a service or set of services. Practically all enterprises, subscribing to services, engage in continuous improvement to some degree, to protect their investment. As suggested in Figure 5.2, the output of continuous improvement, known as *Service Reporting*, feeds back into the other four stages, on an as needed basis, constituting the service lifecycle.

This stage consists of 7 steps, listed as follows[44]:

1. Define what you should measure
2. Define what you can measure
3. Gather the data
4. Process the data
5. Analyze the data
6. Report the information
7. Implement corrective action

Continuous improvement is an excellent management tool as it suggests a means of prioritizing ongoing strategy and design activities.

## Postscript to the Service Management Lifecycle

The objective of the service management lifecycle is to establish a set of "tools of the trade" specifications to assist in the execution of service

---

[44] The 7-step improvement process is defined in the IT Infrastructure Library (ITIL version 3) specification, referenced in endnote 3.

management. As such, the lifecycle represents a set of *best practices* to assist management in focusing on enterprise needs. Even when unexpected events occur, the service manager who adheres to best practices is in good stead. The IT Infrastructure Library (ITIL) listed in the selected reading is a good reference to best practices.

# SERVICE CONSTRAINT MANAGEMENT

A management approach to improving the operation of a manufacturing process or a service system, either of which is constrained from operating at presupposed efficiency, is known as the "Theory of Constraints," an operational methodology developed by Eliyahu Goldratt.[45][46] It is related to the efficiency of value nets and pull models, covered in this section.

## *Constraint Management Concepts*

The philosophy of constraint management is exceedingly simple: find the constraint, also known as the *bottleneck*, in a process or system and fix it. Once the bottleneck is resolved, throughput will improve. In a service system, a bottleneck can prevent a service from being functional, so that constraint management may be necessary for service provisioning. Clearly, services are labor intensive, so that in the consulting or health care businesses, for example, you can't do the work if you don't have the people. Later, we will discuss the virtual workforce, which is an approach to service provisioning.

There is no need to improve every step in a process or system, because that could result in additional problems – such as the buildup of partially-completed inventory at intermediate stages. As soon as the bottleneck is identified and managed successfully, the constraint resolution scenario is repeated. The process would ordinarily continue until the law of diminishing returns kicks in. A constraint may be internal or external to the process or system under evaluation.

## *Constraint Management Process*

The process of constraint management is as straightforward as the concept itself and consists of five easy steps:

---

[45] Dr. Eliyahu M. Goldratt is known as the father of the Theory of Constraints. See www.goldratt.com or www.goldratt.co.uk.
[46] Ricketts (2008) gives a complete treatment of managing service businesses based on the Theory of Constraints.

1.  Identify the constraint.

2.  Decide how to resolve the constraint by focusing on the functions that the constraint is supposed to perform. The constraint should not be resolved by adding tasks that the constraint is not intended to do in the first place. On the other hand, a constraint could be resolved by considering related steps in the process or system.

3.  Align the functioning of other elements to the identified constraint.

4.  Resolve the resolve by off-loading work from that constraint or increasing its capacity.

5.  After a constraint is overcome, return to step 1 to identify additional constraints.

The constraint management process is concerned with the goals of the organization and whatever elements in the service production process that prevent achievement of those goals.

## Bottlenecks

A *bottleneck* is a work center that limits production or service. Bottlenecks occur in systems designed to be well balanced, because operating conditions and workloads customarily change over time in response to external conditions. Everyday examples of systems that develop bottlenecks are hospitals, restaurants, banks, factories, and consulting organizations. An operations or service manager usually deals with a bottleneck by increasing the capacity of the work center causing the constraint or by adjusting the operating procedures or process routing.

In the service community, especially with consulting, bottlenecks can easily occur because of a lack of people with requisite knowledge, skills, and experience. Use of a virtual workforce is a common solution to a service bottleneck.

## Virtual Workforce

A *virtual workforce* is an actual skill group supplemented by additional personnel with matching secondary skill codes. In many cases, an associate's secondary skill is just as relevant as his or her primary skill. This is commonly the case in consulting organizations where the on-demand service workload is heterogeneous, non-repeatable, and unpredictable.

## Drum, Buffer, Rope

An idea that has emanated from constraint management is known as *Drum, Buffer, Rope* (DBR), where the constraint is associated with the abstract notion of a drum – as in "the system operates at the beat of the drum." The *buffer* provides the resource to the drum, and the *rope* implies the abstract concept of a release mechanism for the system based on the pull model. Accordingly, the system is optimized by insuring the buffer component fully supports the drum.

## Thinking Processes

In order to initiate a change operation when a constraint is discovered, a *thinking process* [47] is suggested to answer three questions: (1) What to change; (2) What to change to; and (3) How to cause the change. The five steps in the thinking process are:

1.  Gain agreement on the problem.
2.  Gain agreement on the direction for a solution.
3.  Gain agreement that the solution solves the problem.
4.  Agree to overcome any potential negative ramifications.
5.  Agree to overcome any obstacles to implementation.

As such, the "Theory of Constraints" is a management approach to operational problem resolution.

## Value Nets

A *value net*[48] is a means of capturing business value from the integration of strategy, process, workforce, and technology. Business value is created by shifting from the traditional value-chain model to the value-net model in service systems. Constraint management is applicable to value nets.

In the value-chain model, an organization creates value by adding elements to the finished product at each stage of a production process. In a general sense, raw materials are converted to value in a step-by-step production line. The modern competitive environment, however, requires faster turnaround time and more choices, especially with regard to service management..

---

[47] The "thinking process" is generally regarded as an addendum in professional development courses on the Theory of Constraints.
[48] See Cherbakov, L., et al,, "Impact of service orientation at the business level" in the selected reading.

Successful enterprises currently use value nets in which suppliers and business partners interoperate through information over networks on a demand basis. The relationships between organization, suppliers, business partners, and customers are dynamic and adjust to changing requirements. Value nets are efficient because of the real time combination of services supplied by the key participants – the business, buyers, suppliers, and business partners.

## Goods Models and Service Paradigms

Process efficiency is particularly important to both client and provider in order to achieve a quality service event. Economic efficiency is typically expressed as:

$$E = O/I$$

where efficiency (E), measured in utility, is the quotient of output (O) over input (I). O is the output of the service process, and I is the input to the service process. The provider input normally takes the form of knowledge of the application domain, expertise, infrastructure, and time devoted to service duration. Client input usually takes the form of the person or possession on which the service is to be performed and other types of assets. Service output is manifested in the change of state of the client and provider and an updating of the knowledge bases of both parties.

The manner and form of I and O reveal three paradigms for services processes: I-push, O-pull, and IO-combined. With I-push, production is goods oriented as in the make-store-buy business model. O-pull reflects the service model in which user demand dominates the business process. The IO-combined model captures the notion of service innovation by the provider in response to needs of the client.

Enhanced service quality is achieved through service innovation by the provider based on the specific needs of a particular client. Accordingly, the IO-combined paradigm represents the notion of *service agility* that can be developed through the pull model of business resource mobilization. In a very general sense, an agile service provider is a better service provider.

## The Pull Model for Service Agility

Hagel and Brown[49] have identified the pull model as a means of mobilizing business resources for the upcoming generation of business activities based on mass communications and the Internet. The characteristics of the *pull model*

---

[49] See Hagel, J. and J.S. Brown, *From Push to Pull: Emerging Models for Mobilizing Resources* in the selected reading.

91

are succinctly summarized in the following sentence from the Hagel/Brown web report. "Rather than 'push,' this new approach focuses on 'pull' – creating platforms that help people to mobilize appropriate resources when the need arises." Push models are "script oriented" and thrive in stable environments with little uncertainty. Forecasting, as in demand forecasting, is key in push environments and allows high levels of efficiency to be developed in business processes. Pull models are more amenable to uncertain business conditions that require compressed development times for new goods and services.

Pull models increase value creation for both clients and providers. For clients, pull platforms expand the scope of available resources. For providers, pull platforms enhance the market for their services. In this instance, the term "platform" is intended to imply a framework for providing resources for accommodating service requirements. Pull platforms are associated with the following attributes: uncertain demand, emergent design, decentralized environment, loosely coupled modular construction, and on-demand service provisioning.

Push programs represent top-down activity with the following procedural pattern: design, deploy, execute, monitor, and refine. Pull platforms represent flexibility and agility and focus on the following activities: find, connect, innovate, and reflect.

As such, the pull platform is a loosely coupled set of layers delineated as follows:

Infrastructure
Performance
Creativity

The *infrastructure layer* is concerned with connections (e.g., between client and provider) and the provisioning of resources. The *performance layer* involves technology enablers and social networks. The *creativity layer* deals with the aggregation of resources and the processing of resources.

The pull model represents service architecture at the enterprise level, and could properly be viewed as an *enterprise service architecture.*

## SERVICE QUALITY

Service quality is an involved arrangement of client expectations, client education, business value, and business utility. It is elusive because clients usually cannot assess quality until after a service event has been completed. Service providers present quality as adherence to standard operating procedures. Service clients view service quality based on expectations and value creation

## Service Quality Concepts

In manufacturing, quality particulars are observable and quality is easily determined before the client gets involved. In services, quality turns out to be a social construct dependent upon real or perceived values. With a service, a quality assessment is instantaneously being made at each step in the service delivery process, including appointment and scheduling, service delivery, conclusion, termination, billing, and archiving.

## Client's View of Service Quality

Service quality is determined by a client's expectation of service and the client's perception of the service that is experienced.[50] Expectations are developed by word of mouth, personal needs, and past experience. The service that is delivered is a complex combination of reliability, responsiveness, assurance, empathy, and tangibles.[51] *Reliability* refers to the consistency of service. *Responsiveness* reflects the perception that the provider is willing to provide service. *Assurance* is a measure of the competence of the service provider. *Empathy* is a reflection of the personal attention afforded to clients. *Tangibles* refers to the infrastructure as it is related to the service experience. Certainly, the five attributes of service quality reflect a traditional setting and do not take into account the complications associated with technology driven service provisioning.

## Client Education

One of the primary considerations is the education of the client. With conventional business systems, most employees possess some degree of education in information systems and tacitly develop realistic expectations concerning service delivery. Accordingly, service delivery is usually highly regarded and deemed of high quality. In lesser developed business areas, the professionals are normally unfamiliar with information services and their method of delivery. Obvious examples are healthcare and biology research, in which many of the client personnel have unreasonable expectations based on services rendered to other areas. In many cases, client professionals are unable to relate their specific needs.

---

[50] See Fitzsimmons and Fitzsimmons (2008).
[51] See Metters, King-Metters, Pullman, and Walton (2006).

## Client Interaction

The most visible form of service quality is the manner in which clients interact with their service providers, customarily regarded as *client interaction.* With traditional service events, such as the doctor/patient relationship, service establishments (such as dry cleaning), and telephone reservations, the forms of client interaction are familiar. Technology related forms of interaction, on the other hand, demand a set of ontological categories to sort out the nuances. One such set of categories divides the problem domain into face-to-face contact and face-to-screen contact as follows:

*Face-to-Face Contact*

Technology free
> Exemplified by personal and professional services
> May be technology assisted
> Only the service provider has access to technology, as in health care.

Technology facilitated
> Both client and provider have access to technology

*Face-to-Screen Contact*

Technology mediated
> Access services such as call centers, restaurant reservations, and hotel reservations

Technology generated
> Service provider is replaced with technology, such as ATMs, checkout scanning, airport kiosks, and web services

Client/provider interaction is one of the primary determinants of service quality as evidenced by operational problems associated with offshore call centers.

## Process View of Service Quality

*A service is a process.* This notion is paramount to recognizing the far-reaching importance of service systems as an academic discipline. A service takes input and produces output. In between the input and the output, there exist one or more steps that constitute the service process. Consider a simple medical example. A patient – the client – perceives a situation that requires attention. A contact with a medical provider is made and an appointment is scheduled for a service event. In general, the following three items of information are brought to the service process: the patient per se, a medical history, and the relevant information for the current problem. This is the client/customer input required for a service process. The physician performs the requisite consultation, diagnosis, and resolution that collectively constitute the service process. The output then consists of the diagnosis, prescription, prognosis, and update of the medical records. Additionally, the personal knowledge bases of the patient and physician are enhanced as a result of the service event. Therein lies the quality problem. Service organizations tend to regard the input-process-output paradigm as a functional entity rather than an end-to–end sequence of operations. Where are the problems: blinded view, missing data, and missing steps.[52]

### Enterprise View of Quality

At the enterprise level, service quality is a function of the value proposition for client, so that in a real sense

**Quality = Value** (for customers)

where a service supports business objectives and focuses on business value. The key determinants of business value are transaction costs, usually delineated as follows:

Overall costs of exchange between two parties
Finding and selecting suppliers of services
Negotiating agreements
Costs of consuming services
Governing the relationship with suppliers
Ensuring that commitments are fulfilled

In this book, we recommend a value proposition based on utility and warranty. *Utility* is derived by the client from the characteristics of the service that have a positive effect on the performance of requisite tasks. *Warranty* is derived from the recognition of positive outcomes when provided in needed capacity, continuity, and reliability.[53]

*Utility is what the customer gets and warranty is how it is delivered.*

## E-SERVICES

Every year, businesses spend millions of dollars on their IT infrastructure consisting of hardware, system software, applications, networks, people, and

---

[52] See Nichols (2007).
[53] See ITIL, *Service Strategy* (2007). The Agency and service models were adapted from that report.

other organizational assets. With "on demand" computing, they can plug into the wall, figuratively speaking, and only pay for the IT services they use. The concept is called *utility computing* that is accessed as most public utilities. We are going to name the utility computing concept as **E-Services.** When the time is right, an E-Service utility is a viable option for obtaining computing services.

## E-Services Concepts

The concept of E-Services is the packaging of computer services as a metered facility without up-front costs for IT infrastructure and is commonly used for large-scale computations or peak demands. In the current view of things, an E-Services utility is network based and is dependant upon the Internet as a transport mechanism. In recent years, computing has become the operational medium for business, government, and education and part of everyday life for most people. As with electric utilities, computing utilities have evolved form being a luxury to an everyday necessity.

## E-Service Characteristics

An E-Service utility is characterized by four key factors:[54] necessity, reliability, usability, and scalability. *Necessity* refers to the idea that a preponderance of users depend on the utility to satisfy everyday needs. *Reliability* refers to the expectation that the utility will be available when the user requires it. *Usability* refers to the requirement that the utility is easy and convenient to use – regardless of the complexity of the underlying infrastructure. *Scalability* refers to the fact that the utility has sufficient capacity to allow the users to experience the benefits of an expandable utility that provides economy of scale. Certainly, modern Internet facilities for search operations that engage thousands of servers satisfy these characteristics.

## Utility Computing Services

The notion of "paying for what one uses" is a compelling argument for using E-Services for special or all computing needs. However, the proof of the pudding may in fact be in the details. The key question is whether the service should be based on a metered model or a subscription model. With the *metered model*, the usage is easily measured, monitored, and verified

---

[54] See Rappa (2004).

and lends itself to managerial control on the part of the user. In addition, metering can be applied to differing levels of service. With the *subscription model*, usage is difficult to control and monitor and its adoption is favored by managers more concerned with convenience than with resource control.

For example, water and electricity service commonly use metered service while the plain ordinary telephone system "usually" provides subscription service for local service and metered service for long distance. In the area of computer networks, broadband cable and telephone digital-subscriber line (DSL) rates are normally based on the subscription model. With cable TV, on the other hand, there are usually differing levels of subscription service along with "pay per view" for special services.

One can readily conceptualize a scheme for a typical E-Service customer – nominally assumed to be a small-to-medium-sized business. Office services, such as word and spreadsheet processing, could be subscription-based service and special applications, such as integrated enterprise systems, would be metered service.

### E-Service Architecture

The difference between application services and multi-tenant services may very well be the deciding factor in determining whether metered or subscriber service is the way to go. With *multi-tenant service*, several clients may share the same software with separate data – as in the case of office processing. With *application service*, the service provider supplies one instance of the software per client, thereby lending itself to a form of metered service.

## SUMMARY

There are three forces operating in the sphere of service processes. The first is the use of ICT as an enabler in providing revenue growth, efficiency, and effectiveness for traditional and enhanced services, as well as for conventional business processes. This subject is commonly referred to as information systems. The second is the consulting services domain that provides IT services to external organizations. The third is the use of ICT to manage information systems and services, which is a field of endeavor known as IT Services Management. Briefly said, it is the use of computers to manage the enterprise and also to manage itself.

The notion of service has its origin in ancient times and was understood to mean "one person doing something for another." With the advent of civilization and industrialization, the definition of service was implicitly extended to encompass "one person doing something for an organization," usually in the form of employment. At this stage, specialization and entrepreneurship kicked in with all of their rights and privileges resulting in what we now recognize as the service organization.

Information is a critical asset in the operation of an enterprise and in the everyday lives of individuals. In a figurative sense, information is the grease that allows the components to work together. IT is employed to handle the information needed to manage the operations of an enterprise and to aid in making effective decisions. Thus, IT is a service to the enterprise, regardless if that enterprise is concerned with production processes, service operations, government reporting, professional services, scientific services, technical services, or personal services.

There are several aspects of IT services that can vary between organizations. Examples are commonplace: computer operations, network management, hardware and software acquisition, system analysis and design, software design, software development, information systems integration, and call center and help desk operation and management. This is a representative set of tasks necessary for sustaining an IT services organization. You can do them yourself; you can have another business entity help you do them; or you can have a business entity do them for you. In the latter two cases, the business process is known as *IT service outsourcing*.

The service lifecycle consists of five important elements, listed as follows: Service Strategy, Service Design, Service Transition, Service Operation, and Continuous Improvement.

A management approach to improving the operation of a manufacturing process or a service system, either of which is constrained from operating at presupposed efficiency, is known as the "Theory of Constraints." The philosophy of constraint management is exceedingly simple: find the constraint, also known as the *bottleneck*, in a process or system and fix it. Once the bottleneck is resolved, throughput will improve. In a service system, a bottleneck can prevent a service from being functional, so that constraint management may be necessary for service provisioning. Clearly, services are labor intensive, so that in the consulting or health care businesses, for example, you can't do the work if you don't have the people.

Service quality is a complex arrangement of client expectations, client education, business value, and business utility. It is elusive because clients usually cannot assess quality until after a service event has been completed. Service providers present quality as adherence to standard operating procedures. Service clients view service quality based on expectations and value creation

Every year, businesses spend millions of dollars on their IT infrastructure consisting of hardware, system software, applications, networks, people, and other organizational assets. With "on demand" computing, they can plug into the wall, figuratively, speaking, and only pay for the IT services they use. The concept is called *utility computing* that is accessed as most public utilities. We have named the utility computing concept **E-Services.**

# KEY TERMINOLOGY

The reader should be familiar with the following terms in the context in which they were used in the chapter.

Agency model
Application service
Best practices
Bottleneck
Client arrangement
Continuous improvement
Creativity layer
Drum, buffer, rope
E-service
Information technology
IT consulting
IT service outsourcing
Multi-tenant service
Organization
People
Performance layer
Provider arrangement
Pull model
Service agility
Service componentization
Service design
Service directory
Service element
Service lens
Service life cycle
Service operation
Service orchestration
Service provisioning
Service quality
Service strategy
Service transition

Strategy document
Technology
Theory of constraints
Utility
Value net
Virtual workforce
Warranty

## A FEW GOOD QUESTIONS[55]

1) The three forces operating in the service domain are: _____,
_____, and _____.
2) Who pays for the service and how it is organized is known as _____
_____.
3) A _____ is an organizational entity for instantiating
services.
4) The _____ is an explicit or implicit specification of the
interactions between components.
5) A service strategy is recorded in a _____.
6) A constraint is a _____.
7) Quality = _____.
8) _____ is what the customer gets and _____
is how it is delivered.
9) The packaging of computer services is known as _____.

## SELECTED READING

Cherbakov, L., et al., "Impact of service orientation at the business level",
*IBM Systems Journal,* Vol. 44, No. 4, 2005.

Fitzsimmons, J.A. and M.J. Fitzsimmons, *Service Management: Operations,
Strategy, Information Technology* (6th Edition), New York: McGraw-Hill/
Irwin, 2008.

Ganek, A. and K. Kloeckner, "An overview of IBM Service Management,"
*IBM Systems Journal,* Vol. 46, No. 3, 2007.

---

[55]Answers: (1) ICT as an enabler, consulting services, ICT to manage information
systems and services; (2) service provisioning; (3) component; (4) service
orchestration; (5) strategy document; (6) bottleneck; (7) value; (8) utility, warranty;
(9) E-service.

Hagel, J. and J.S. Brown, *From Push to Pull: Emerging Models for Mobilizing Resources,* www.edgeperspectives.com, 2007.

Heizer, J. and B. Render, *Operations Management* (8<sup>th</sup> Edition), Upper Saddle River, NJ: Pearson Prentice-Hall, 2006.

Hurwitz, J., Bloor, R., Baroudi, C., and M. Kaufman, *Service Oriented Architecture for Dummies,* Hoboken, NJ: Wiley Publishing, Inc., 2007.

itSMF, *An Introductory Overview of ITIL® V3,* itSMF Ltd,, 2007.

ITIL, *Service Strategy,* London: The Stationary Office, 2007.

Metters, R., King-Metters, K., Pullman, M., and S Walton, *Successful Service Operations Management* (2e), Boston: Thomson Course Technology, 2006.

Nichols, M., "Quality Tools in a Service Environment, " www.ASQ.org, 2007.

Rappa, M.A., "The utility business model and the future of computing services," *IBM Systems Journal,* Vol. 43, No. 1, 2004.

Ricketts, J.A., *Reaching the Goal: How Managers Improve a Services Business Using Goldratt's Theory of Constraints,* Upper Saddle River, NJ: IBM Press/Pearson plc, 2008.

Wikipedia, *Software as a Service,* www.wikipedia.com, 2008.

Wikipedia, *Theory of Constraints,* www.wikipedia.com, 2008.

Wikipedia, *Thinking Processes,* www.wikipedia.com, 2008.

# 6

# Service Technology

Services are ubiquitous, as suggested by Table 6.1 that gives an inclusive list of service systems, where a *service system* is a collection of resources and economic entities, capable of engaging in or supporting one or more service events. Even though the list is diverse, each system has one element in common: the clients and providers have to communicate even though one or both of them might be a computer. Communication means messages and that seems to be a good place to begin a chapter on service technology. On another front, practically everything in our existence is related to services, since most of the gross national product is derived from services and most people are involved in services in everyday life. It is generally felt that the association of services with technology will also make things function more effectively and more efficiently – at least most of us hope that is the case. The major focus will be on enterprises, such as business, government, and education, and on facilities that provide services that affect a lot of people – like the Internet. We are moving into the world of computers and technology.

## SERVICE TECHNOLOGY CONCEPTS

The basis of service technology is really straightforward. Clients and providers communicate with one another through the use of messages and contracts, and in many areas of service, the communication involves

103

information and communications technology (ICT). A client and a provider can be tightly coupled, as when a patient is sitting in front of the doctor and they are having a give-and-take conversation, or loosely coupled, as when you send a request to someone via email and receive a response at some undetermined time in the future. In the former case, the client and provider are communicating in a *synchronous mode* without technology, and in the later case, they are communicating in an *asynchronous mode* with the use of technology. The *contract* is a formal or informal agreement that delineates the service in which the client and provider

| *Singular Service Systems* | *Multiple Service Systems* |
|---|---|
| • People <br> • Families <br> • Businesses <br> • Cities <br> • Nations <br> • Hospitals <br> • Universities <br> • Call Centers <br> • Data Centers | • Professional Associations <br> • Disciplinary Associations <br> • Government Agencies <br> • Political Action Committees <br> • Non-Governmental Organizations <br> • Non-Profits Organizations <br> • Foundations <br> • Online Communities <br> • The Internet |

*Table 6.1 Types of Service Systems (adapted from Spohrer, J., 2007, p. 77).*

are engaged. The contract can be a formal document, an informal agreement, or be implicit in the activity under consideration. Another view of a contract is that it is a specification of how to use a service and what to expect from a service.

## Messaging Basics

Every service (perhaps, we should say every "service application" or application of a service) requires at least one message, and each message requires a context, which gives meaning to the interaction. Entities that participate in a service-oriented message are called the message sender, the message intermediary, and the message receiver. When you fire up your Internet browser, for example, and enter a World Wide Web address, such as www.ibm.com, the browser sends a message to the IBM server somewhere out in cyberspace. The browser, acting as a client on your behalf, is the message sender. The IBM web site is the message receiver. When IBM sends its home page back to be rendered for you by your browser, the roles are reversed; it is the sender and your browser is the receiver, and the Internet is the message intermediary.

The *message* is the glue that ties a service together.

## Conceptual Model of Service Orientation

The most profound aspect of service science is that a *service is a process*, as suggested by the following message pattern:

1. A client sends a message to a service provider.

2. The provider performs the required action and returns a message to the client.

The focus is on the data that is transmitted and not on the communications medium, which can take the form of a human interaction or a computer-based message. The context for the message can be embedded in the message or it can be inherent in the way that the service provider is addressed. The importance of context is suggested by the cartoon floating around where two dogs are seated in front of a computer screen. One dog says to the other, "On the Internet, no one knows you're a dog." Two good rules of thumb are that in face-to-face services, interpersonal communication provides the context. In human-to-computer services, the context must be inherent in the message. For example, entering "Boston Red Sox" into your browser to get the score of the last World Series game is probably going to generate a lot of miscellaneous information in which you are not interested, because you provided no context.

Initially, it is useful to recognize that we are operating at two levels: the service level and the message level. At the *service level*, the message entity that receives the message is the service provider, and in the case of a computer, it is regarded simply as the **service**. At the *message level*, there is some choreography involved with providing a service, as demonstrated by the above two-step interaction. In fact, a service may involve the interchange of several messages.

## Enterprise Service Technology

Many modern enterprises (i.e., business, government, education) provide computer support to internal users, clients, business partners, and other enterprise entities. The facilities are usually integrated into administrative, product development, supply chain, or customer relationship operations. Because those services, consisting of computer applications and associated procedures, are tried, tested, and dependable, it would be prudent to use them as building blocks for new enterprise applications.

The concept that underlies service orientation is that it is simply more efficient and reliable to identify the bundled services and package them as reusable components than it would be to rewrite them. Bundled services could then be used by other services, so that information system applications could be developed more rapidly and enable the enterprise to be more responsive to external conditions. This practice is the basis of web services that are introduced later in this chapter and covered in detail in the next chapter.

A typical business function that lends itself to componentization is to perform a credit check on a prospective customer before confirming a large order. Such a check is normally performed in different operational systems in an enterprise. After restructuring, the credit check software is packaged as a single business component and exposed as an enterprise service for use by other enterprise services.

The technique of service componentization is not exactly something that is totally new to the world. Before the advent of ICT, it was known as specialization, where one person processed the orders and another person did the credit checks.

### Service Science Abstraction

Service science is an abstraction of service systems in the same way that computer science is an abstraction of computer-based information systems. The procedure, in both cases, is to take a piece of an existing system and put it under the microscope of academic scrutiny. In this particular instance, we are taking a service centric view of enterprise systems, where traditional enterprise functions are candidates for being packaged as enterprise services.

# SERVICE MESSAGING

When two service entities are engaged in communication, they are regarded as being *connected*. An enterprise has two options for developing a service connection:

1. Message entity to message entity (ME → ME)

2. Message entity to enterprise entity (ME →EE)

The first option, denoted by ME → ME, refers to either a client-to-provider or a provider-to-client communication. The second option denoted by ME →EE refers to a client-to-many-provider communication. The notion of connectedness is needed for an appreciation of message patterns and topologies, covered in the next section. For example, the ME → ME option may represent the case where an order-processing application sends a message to a shipping application to have an item shipped to a customer. The ME → EE option might represent the case where an airline's flight operations application sends a message to other involved computer applications, such as scheduling and reservations, when a plane has taken off.

## Message Characterization

Both of the applications in the previous section would use an asynchronous forward-only type of messaging. A second major type of messaging is request-reply messaging, characterized as follows:

1. Reference an Internet service.
2. Wait for it to return something.
3. Act on the returned information.

This is the model that is used with the Internet, and the one used with most service applications.

## Message Patterns

A *message pattern* is a model of service communications that represents a single connection between one sender and one receiver. There are three basic patterns representing message traffic that can go only one way, both ways but only one way at a time, and both ways simultaneously.

The one-way message flow is regarded as a "fire-and-forget-it" send, also known as *simplex* and *datagram* communications service in the computer community. The second model is the request/reply model, known as *half duplex*, wherein only one participant communicates at a time as with the walkie-talkie type of interaction. In the final model, called *full duplex*, both messaging participants can send messages at the same time, as in an ordinary telephone conversation. Clearly, messaging can take on different patterns depending upon the operational environment used for technical support.

## Message Structure

In its most simple form, a message is a string of characters encoded using standardized coding methods commonly employed in computer and information technology. Messages have a uniform format consisting of a header and a body. The *header* primarily concerns addressing and includes the address of the sender and the receiver. In the request/reply message pattern, the return address is picked up from the message header for the response portion of the transaction. The *body* of the message contains the information content of the message and because it is intended only for the receiver, is not usually regarded during message transmission.

The manner in which messages are structured is similar to the way that letters are handled by the postal service. The outside of the envelope contains addressing information and the insides are handled as private information.

## Message Topology

*Message topology* refers to the manner in which messages are sent between messaging participants, and not necessarily to the communication techniques used to send them. The most widely used form of communication is known as *point-to-point* using any of the message patterns given above. Usually, point-to-point implies the request/reply message pattern where the reply address is picked up from the message header. A variation to point-to-point is *forward-only point-to-point* where a message reply is not expected.

The popularity of the Internet and the World Wide Web has grown exponentially and resulted in a need to perform load balancing at web sites. Whereas in the recent past, an enterprise needed only a couple of web servers, presently a collection of servers, known as a *server farm*, is required. Accordingly, a messaging intermediary is required to route messages on a dynamic basis as demanded by the message load. The *brokered* topology, as suggested by Figure 6.1, supports this environment.

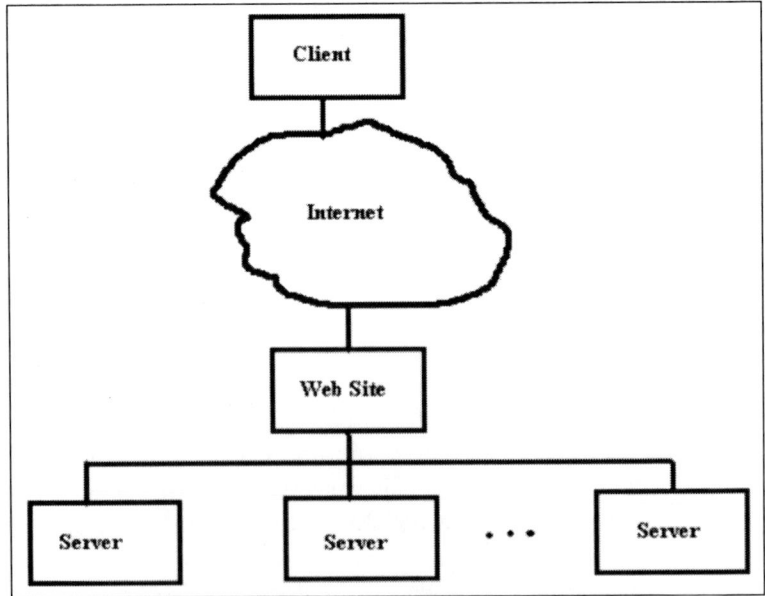

*Figure 6.1 Brokered Topology.*

## Message Interactions

An observer from outer space would take a look at messaging and conclude that it is a microcosm of modern business – there is a lot of handshaking going on. In many, if not most, cases of messaging, the sending participant needs to know that the receiving participant is listening before the real message is transmitted. It is something like the following:

Sender: Are you listening?
Receiver: Yes.
Sender: Are you Gregory Charles Cabot?
Receiver: Yes.
Sender: You've just won one million dollars.

OK, it's a bit contrived and also, it's messaging at the service level. There is also handshaking going on at the message level, which we are going to cover in the next section.

Figure 6.2 gives as example from instant messaging at the service level that demonstrates message interactions.[56] In this instance, **User A** is sending a message to **User B** who responds to **User A.** The interaction consists of four distinct messages, delineated as follows:

Message 1: User A logs on to the instant messaging (IM) server. The expected response is that the IM server will return a message with the users in A's group that are currently logged on. The message goes from User A through the Internet to the IM server.

Message 2: The IM server sends a message to User A with the members that are logged on. The message goes from the IM server to User A.

Message 3 : User A sends a message, such as "Hi User B," to User B. The message goes from User A through the Internet to the IM server. The IM server then sends the message through the Internet to User B.

Message 4: User B responds with a message, such as "Hi yourself," to User A. The message goes through the Internet to the IM server. Then the IM server sends the message through the Internet to User A.

Most people would regard this interaction sequence in which User A sends an instant message to User B as a service and B's response to A as another service.

---

[56] This example is adapted from Van Slyke and Bélanger (2003), p. 110.

Popping up a level, the service provider is the instant messaging server and users A and B are clients.

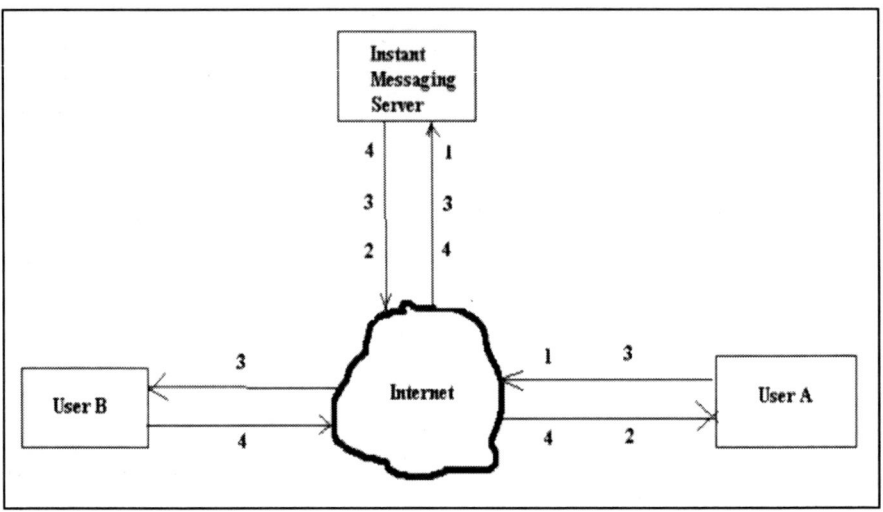

*Figure 6.2  Instant Messaging Example.*

# SERVICES ON THE INTERNET AND THE WORLD WIDE WEB

A service that takes place on the Internet and the World Wide Web is called a *web service*.[57]  A web service is a process in which the provider and client interact to produce a value; it is a pure service.   The only difference between a web service and medical provisioning, for example, is that in the former case, the client and provider are computer systems.  Ordinary email is a web service.  Requesting a home page from a provider's web site is a web service.  Sending an instant message over the Internet is a web service. Almost anything you can think of doing on the web would be called a web service.  However, there is another category of service known as a Web Service. Note that Web Service is a proper noun.  It is a formal process, developed by organizations such as Microsoft, IBM, and others, for conducting business over the Internet.  It is covered separately.

---

[57] There is another definition for web services that is slightly different.   Cerami (2002) states, "A web service is any service that is available over the Internet, uses a standardized XML messaging system, and is not tied to one operating system or programming language." The subject of XML is covered in this chapter.

## *Simple Mail Model*

The most pervasive web service computer application on the Internet is electronic mail, commonly known as email. It is used in two ways: (1) To communicate between email clients; and (2) To provide a record that communication has taken place – or at least, to show that an attempt at communication has taken place. Clearly, email is designed to be a person-to-person endeavor.[58] There are two scenarios that are relevant to web services.

In the first scenario, we have a desktop personal computer (PC) operating as an email client – referred to as a PC running an email client – from which the end user sends and receives email. The email client is connected to incoming and outgoing email servers through a local-area network[59] or a dial-up, broadband cable, or DSL connection[60] to an Internet service provider (ISP) that is in turn connected to the email servers, as suggested by Figure 6.3. Email messages are normally managed locally, which means they are downloaded and stored on the end user's computer. When the end user decides to access email messages, he or she presses a receive button and incoming messages, stored on the incoming email server, are transferred to the local email client. Similarly, when the end user constructs a message for sending, a send key is pressed to transfer it to the outgoing email server for subsequent forwarding over the Internet. An email client uses push technology to send email messages and pull technology to receive email messages.

---

[58] Email is a person-to-person construct but requires a slight interpretation. A sender can send a message to a mailing list; however, each individual send operation is still a person-to-person operation.

[59] A local area network (LAN) is a computer network that connects computers in a small physical area, such as a building, office, or a home.

[60] Digital Subscriber Line (DSL) service is a high-speed data connection available through the telephone company usually for for Internet connectivity.

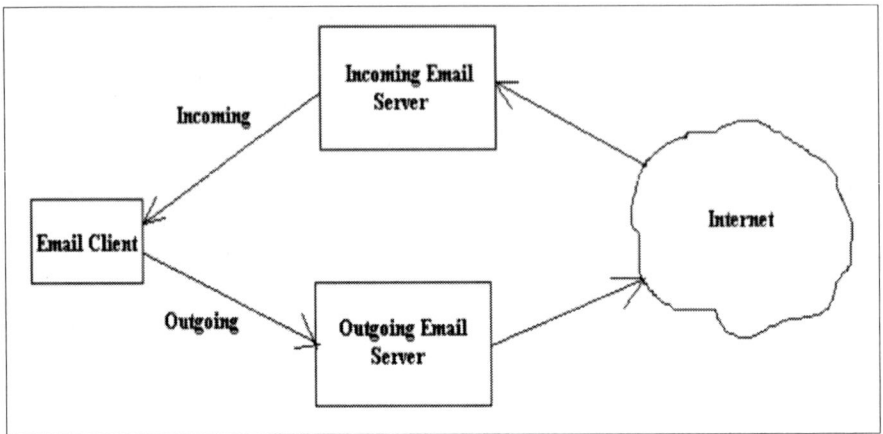

***Figure 6.3 Email Client Connected to Email Servers.***

In the second scenario, we again have an email client for message management. The email client, however, is connected to an email-service server via the Internet through a local browser. The service access point is an account set up on an Internet service portal,[61] as shown in Figure 6.4. A web based email account is used in the same manner as in the local scenario, except that the email server is remote.

The concept of remote service server is also a platform for other web applications, such as word processing and spreadsheet operations. A remote service server that provides application functionality is known as an *application service provider*, and exists as an alternative to purchasing infrequently used software.

---

[61] A service portal is a single point of access on the Internet, such as the Google™ and Yahoo™ search engines.

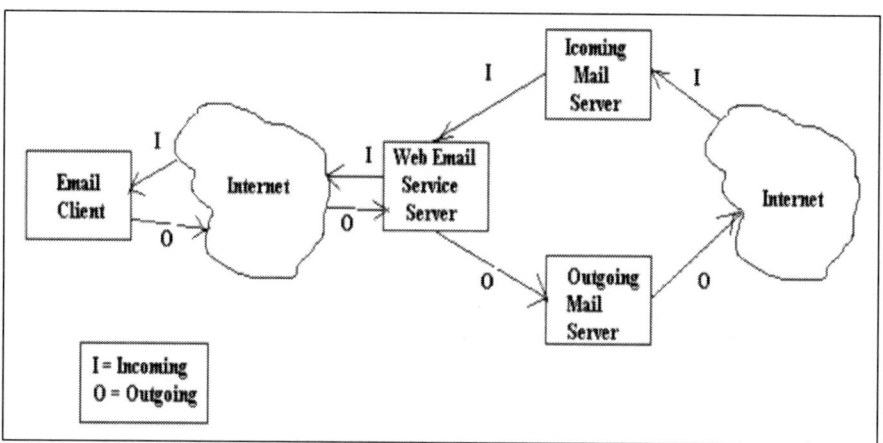

*Figure 6.4 Web Service Email Configuration*

## Web Services Model

When addressing a web service, there is a certain way that most people go about doing things. It's not entirely clear whether the web service architecture determines how people use the web or, the other way around, whether the architecture of the web reflects how people use it. We are calling it a generic web services model.

Imagine the following scenario. You're interested in purchasing a pair of running shoes and don't know any brands or web sites. So what do you do? You point your browser to a search engine, such as Google™, enter the words "running shoes" in the search window and click the "search" button or press the enter key. Your message is sent to Google's web server that searches an index of key words, created beforehand, and makes a list of appropriate web sites, just for you. The web server then prepares your list in a language called HTML[62] and sends it back to your browser over the Internet. The browser then renders the HTML statements into a readable form, as shown in Figure 6.5. Voila! You've experienced the first element in the web services model. It's known as *discovery*. The service process was accomplished without regard to time, distance, or the kind of computer and software you have.

Each of the entries (known as a "hit") on the running-shoe list gives a brief description and a *hyperlink*[63] with which to obtain more definitive

---

[62] HTML stands for HyperText Markup Language.

[63] A hyperlink is a reference to more information. A hyperlink is "hot" if the cursor changes from an arrow to a hand when you move the cursor over it. If you click on a hot link, your browser is directed to another web site associated with the entry you clicked.

information. This process reflects the second element in the web services model, and it is known as *description*. Various enterprises have web sites and associated web pages containing descriptive information of interest. In a separate operation, the organization behind the search engine searches the web sites in cyberspace and prepares indexes for fast retrieval.

If your goal is information, then this is perhaps as far as you will go with this example. If you are going to make a purchase over the web using an appropriate site, then the next step is to *bind* to that web site and go through an interactive process for selection, payment, and delivery. Each step in the bind process requires additional web services, so that a web service is essentially a cascading series of other web services.

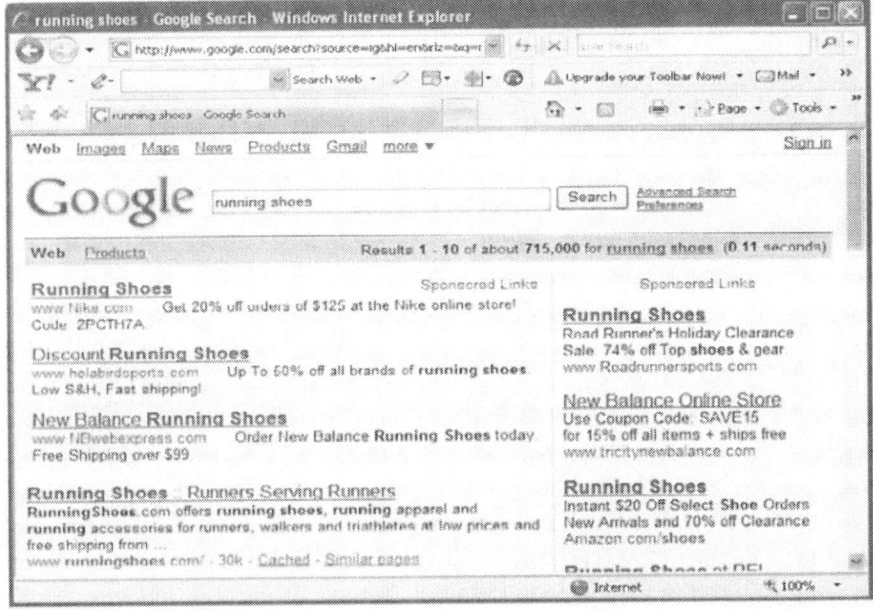

*Figure 6.5 Sample Web Service Request.*

A variety of tools and techniques are required for a successful implementation of web services architecture. Whenever there is a service, there is communication; and whenever there is communication, there are messages. Whenever there is a message, there is a context so that the intent of the service can be sustained. These elements are present in one form or another in all services, ranging from the more straightforward human interaction to the operation of a sophisticated enterprise computer applications.

## *HyperText Transfer Protocol*

*Hyper Text Transfer Protocol* (HTTP) is a collection of rules and procedures for transferring messages between computers over the World Wide Web. Without HTTP, the web would not be the revolutionary phenomena that it is today. But, between computers, you ask, can that be correct? Yes it is. When you make a service request over the web, your entry goes through your browser before it goes over the Internet.[64] Here's how.

When you fire up your browser, you are initiating the execution of a program that runs on your personal computer, workstation, personal digital assistant (PDA), cell phone, terminal – or whatever you choose to use. Now that computing device is performing a service for you in the sense that you can now do things you could not possibly do without it. In fact, you could run all manner of programs, such as productivity software that does word processing, without any information leaving or entering your local environment. As far as the Internet is concerned, however, essentially nothing has happened. You type a URL[65] into your browser window and press the enter key, and then things start to happen. This is when HTTP gets into the act.

Your browser prepares a message called a HTTP request, such as[66]

```
GET /index.html HTTP/1.1
Host: www.example.com
```

and sends it over the Internet to the web server of the "example.com" web site somewhere out in cyberspace. The web server responds in turn to the return address obtained from your message header with

```
HTTP/1.1 200 OK
  Date: Mon, 02 Dec 2007 12:38:34 GMT
  Server: Apache/1.3.27 (Unix)  (Red-Hat/Linux)
  Last-Modified: Wed, 08 Jan 2003 23:11:55 GMT
  Etag: "3f80f-1b6-3e1cb03b"
  Accept-Ranges: bytes
```

---

[64] With respect to terminology, the use of the term Internet in this instance is correct. Remember, the Internet is an information highway that services email, chat, web services, and other applications. Everything is a service including the Internet, the World Wide Web, your browser, and a search engine – to name only a few.

[65] URL stands for Uniform Resource Locator, such as www.example.com.

[66] The examples are adapted from Wikipedia (see selected reading).

```
        Content-Length: 155
        Connection: close
        Content-Type: text/html; charset=UTF-8
```

This response message is followed by a blank line and then the requested information that represents the contents of the file (usually the default file, such as **index.html**) from the site specified in the HTTP get request. The information content of the response message might take the form (highly unlikely but possible):

```
<html>
    <head>
        <title>Hello World</title>
    </head>
    <body>
        <h1>Hello World</h1>
        <par>
        Greetings from Cyberspace
        </par>
    </body>
</html>
```

which would be rendered by your browser somewhat as displayed in Figure 6.6. The text is presented in a well-known language peculiar to the web and known as HyperText Markup Language (HTML). It is introduced in the next section.

The *HyperText Transfer Protocol* has additional verbs, such as POST, PUT, and DELETE, that facilitate the transfer of messages between a client computer and a server computer.

## HYPERTEXT MARKUP LANGUAGE

Aside from the Internet information super highway and the idea of linking information pages together (i.e., the World Wide Web), probably the coolest thing that has ever happened in the over-hyped world of computers is the realization that it is possible to send a document from one computer to another and have that document displayed on the receiving end in a reasonable form without regard to the brand and model of computer, kind of software, time of day, and location. This amazing feat – and it is truly that – is possible because of hypertext markup language (HTML), as introduced in the previous section. We are interested in HTML for two important reasons.

First, it is a useful thing to know something about, as long as you don't get hung up in the details.

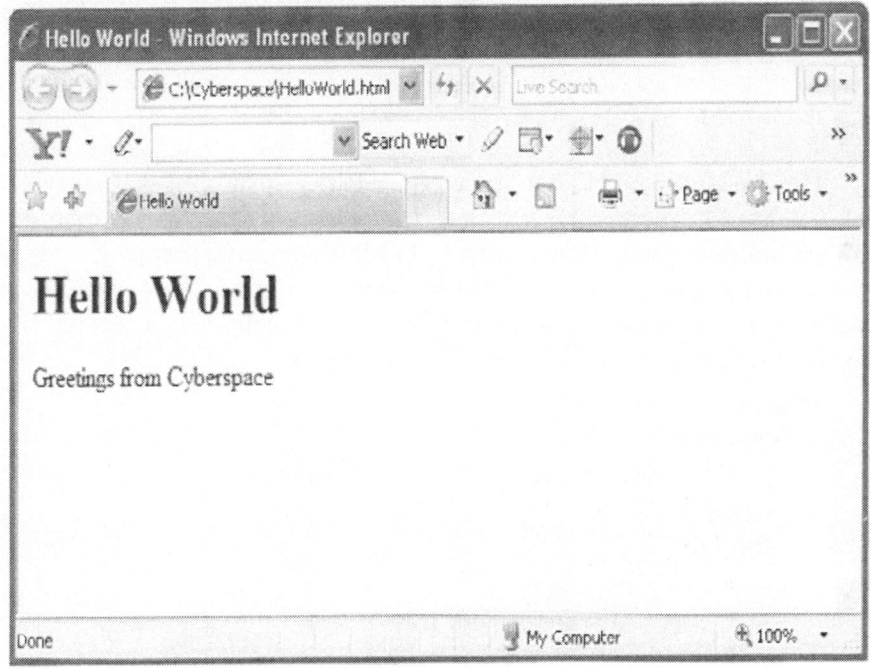

***Figure 6.6 Hello World from Cyberspace.***

Secondly, HTML is a forerunner to Extensible Markup Language (XML) that is a technology for sending messages between services.

## HTML Documents

To start off, an HTML document is nothing more than a bunch of characters that someone has entered into a text editor or a word processor and saved as a file on a computer employed as a web server. When you request an answer from a web site, such as the one and only www.ibm. com, the corresponding web server goes to a default file named **index. html**, retrieves the HTML file, and sends it back to your browser for rendering on your computer's display. It is someone's job to put the right stuff into **index.html**, and that stuff should be written in HTML. Now the file named **index.html** might have links to other pages that are returned in a similar manner when you click on them. Those links are referred to as *hot links*, because we get some action when we click on them – as we just mentioned. You can even put programs into an HTML document. These programs are executed by your browser resulting in some visual or audio activity on the receiving end. The active behavior can result in a wide variety of audio, video, and data-oriented interactive forms.

## Tags

The basis of an HTML is a tag, such as **<html>**, that provides information to the receiving browser. In the case of **<html>**, for example, the tag indicates the beginning of an HTML document. Actually, a tag is only a strong suggestion, since each browser has a mind of its own. Most tags have an enclosing tag, such as **</html>**, that delineates a section of a document, such as in the following HTML snippet:

```
<html>
    <head>
        <title>University of the United States</title>
    </head>
    <body>
        •
        •    --- The good stuff goes here
        •
    </body>
</html>
```

Tags give an HTML document structure and information on page rendering; they do not give meaning. We will use XML for that.

## Discovery

One of the key aspects of web page design is to facilitate discovery whereby clients can find services. Search engine companies use a technique known as "web crawling" in which a program called a *web crawler* or a *bot* (for robot) crawls through web pages following hyperlinks to build indexes for subsequent search operations. Without additional information, all words in a web page are treated the same. You can add additional information to the "head" section to increase the fidelity of searching and increase the chances that a user will navigate to your web site.

This is where the **<meta>** tag comes in. With the meta tag, web page designers commonly supply three types of descriptive items: a list of keywords, a description, and the name of the web page owner – sometimes the name of an organization and sometimes an author. Search bots use this information when building indexes. The following example depicts the use of meta tags:

```
<html>
  <head>
    <title>Savannah Motor Works</title>
    <meta name="keywords" content="Porsche, Mercedes, BMW">
    <meta name="description" content="The south's most prestigious
                      performance car dealership">
    <meta name="author" content="Gregory Cabot">
  </head>
  <body>
    •
    •
    •
  </body>
</html>
```

Actually, there are no predefined meta tags in HTML, so a web page designer can create them to satisfy a particular need. The meta tag demonstrates a tag without an enclosing tag.

### Document Elements

The HTML language has an extensive vocabulary that is a subject in its own right. A brief subset of HTML features is covered here as a forerunner to Extensible Markup Language (XML) that is used to construct messages between clients and service providers. Some of the most commonly used document elements are <h1> through <h6>, <p>, <b>, <i>, <br>, and <hr>, which represent headings, paragraph, bold face, italics, blank line, and horizontal rule, respectively. Several of these elements are depicted in the following script that is rendered in Figure 6.7:

```
<html>
  <head>
    <title>My First Novel</title>
  </head>
  <body bgcolor="yellow">
    <h1 align="center">The Car</h1>
    <p align="center"> <i>by</i> </p>
```

119

```
        <p align="center"> <b>Gregory Cabot</b></p>
        <p> My uncle gave me my first car. It was a 1939 Chevy
            with fluid
                drive.  It had a flat tire and the brakes didn't work.
                It also
                had a  broken window.
        </p>
        <p> My father taught me how to do the repairs and I had to
            do them.
                Afterwards, I didn't like the car and sold it for $50.
        </p>
        <hr>
        <p align="center">The End</p>
    </body>
</html>
```

Of course, complete comprehension is not necessary or even expected. However, the key point has been made that HTML is a powerful tool in the construction and communication of web-based documents.

## Dynamic Linking

Dynamic linking refers to the access of one web page from within another and also the capability of bouncing between sections on the same page. A hyperlink is used to link to another page, and it requires the use of the <a> tag as follows:

<a href="http://www.microsoft.com">Click here to get Microsoft</a>

The first step is to embed the dynamic link in a web page and have it rendered. In this example, the phrase "Click to get Microsoft" would be rendered as a hot link, which means that the cursor changes to a hand when the mouse pointer passes over it. The link to www.microsoft.com is "under the covers," so to speak. When you click on the hot link, your browser is directed to the specified web site. Here is a sample HTML script that demonstrates the use of dynamic linking:

```
<html>
    <head>
        <title>Dynamic Linking</title>
    </head>
    <body>
```

```
<a href="http://www.microsoft.com">Click here to get
Microsoft</a><br>
<a href="http://www.ibm.com">Click to get IBM</a><br>
<a href="http://www.cisco.com">Click to get Cisco</a><br>
    </body>
  </html>
```

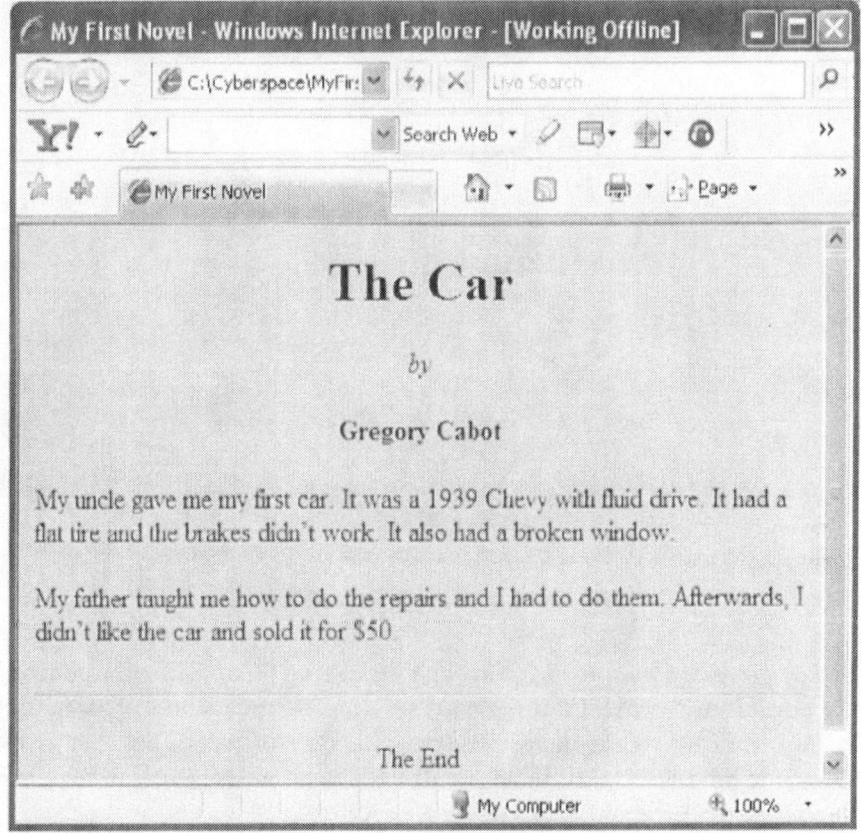

***Figure 6.7 Rendering of a document demonstrating several HTML tags.***

The initial rendering of this script is given in Figure 6.8 along with the dynamic link to a downstream web page. Using a related technique, it is possible to link to sections within the same HTML document. However, we are moving outside of the scope of service science.

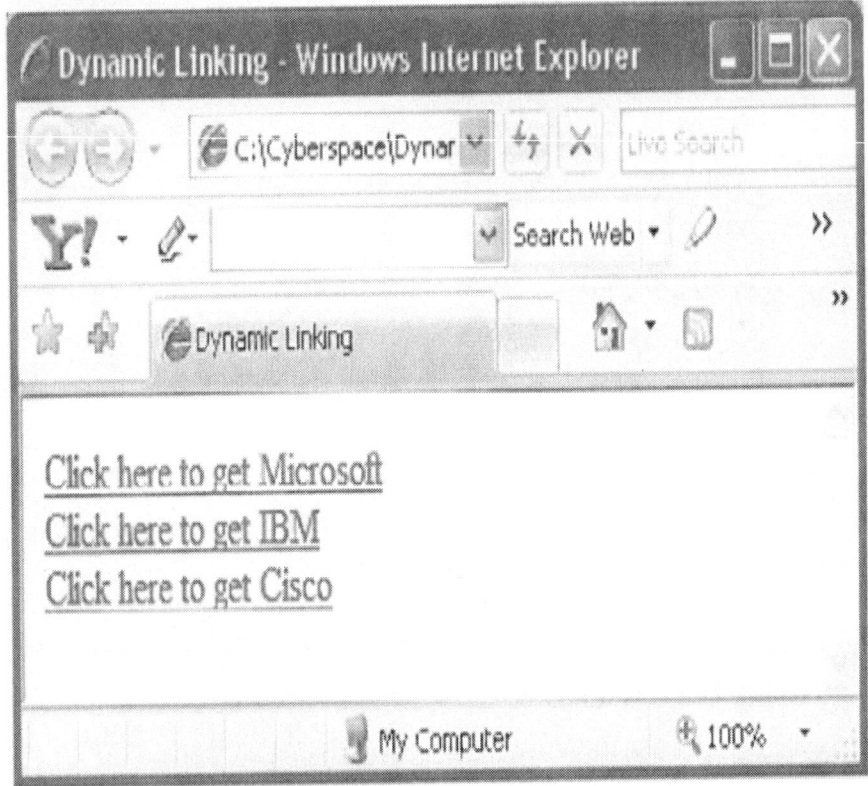

*Figure 6.8 Dynamic Linking.*

The key point has been made. Through messaging in an ICT environment, it is possible to invoke informational services independently of time and distance. HTML is the major player in this type of messaging, but as we move on to advanced forms of service development, we are going to require a more sophisticated tool. XML fills this need.

## EXTENSIBLE MARKUP LANGUAGE

To put the virtues of HTML and XML into perspective, we can properly say that HTML is used to describe web pages and XML is used to describe information. XML stands for eXtensible Markup Language. Both languages use markup, a term that ostensibly is intended to imply that someone prepares a document and then incorporates descriptive elements to suggest how the document should look when displayed *or* to communicate the intended meaning of the document. With XML, markup gives semantic information as suggested by the following script:

```
<?xml version="1.0" ?>
<library>
    <library_name>Pleasure Books</ library_name>
    <book>
        <title>The DaVinci Code</title>
        <author>Dan Brown</author>
    </book>
    <book>
        <title>The Secret Servant</title>
        <author>Daniel Silva</author>
    </book>
</library>
```

We will call the semantic information "tags" as we did with HTML, even though XML specialists refer to them as "element type names." An XML document must contain a prolog and at least one enclosing document element. In the above example, the following statement is the prolog:

```
<?xml version="1.0" ?>and the enclosing document element is:
<library>
    •
    •
    •
</library>
```

This is an example of a main element that must be present in all XML documents. It is often referred to as the *root element*, and it is the characteristic that gives an XML document a hierarchical structure. All opening tags in XML, such as **<book>**, must have closing tags, such as **</book>**. With XML, we can make up our own tags, since we are using the language to describe information that has a specific meaning.

### Rendering an XML Document

Even though an XML document, by definition, is intended for communication, we can display the contents in a particular form by using a stylesheet. To use a stylesheet, we have to extend the prolog with a statement of the form:

```
<?xml:stylesheet href="library.css" type="text/css" ?>
```

and develop a stylesheet description file, named **library.css** in this example, that would have descriptive content, such as the following:

```
library_name {
                display: block;
                font: bold 24pt;
}
title {
        margin-top: 20px;
        display: block;
        font: italic 18pt;
}
author {
                display: block;
                font: 12pt;
}
```

A rendering of the XML document with the **library**.css stylesheet file, both embedded in the above text, is given in Figure 6.9. In fact, the HTML itself can be defined using the XML language. At one time, most computer people thought that XML would replace HTML, but it didn't happen. HTML was too deeply engrained into the Internet and the World Wide Web.

*Figure 6.9 Rendering of an XML document.*

## XML Attributes

Attributes are everything. In the universe of interactive behavior, communication between entities is largely governed by the characteristics of the subjects under consideration. In an XML document, the most noteworthy attribute of an item of information element is its associated XML tag.

There are a few good rules that must be observed in the construction of valid XML tags. Five of the most important are: (1) XML tags are case sensitive; (2) An opening XML tag must have a closing tag; (3) Content described by an XML tag set must be nested – hence the hierarchical structure of an XML document; (4) XML tags may contain only letters, numbers, underscore, dot, and hyphen characters – the first of which must be a letter or an underscore; and (5) An XML tag name must not start with the letters "xml".

Structure engenders semantic flexibility, allowing us to add descriptive and searchable attributes to an opening tag, such as in the following example:

```
<security level="Top Secret"> Eyes Only</security>
```

where "level" is an attribute and "Top Secret" is its value. Attribute content, such as

```
level="Top Secret"
```

in this instance, need not be defined beforehand and could be included in the data alone. It is a good practice to use attributes in order to avoid ambiguity. In this example, **level** is the *attribute name*, and **Top Secret** is the *attribute value*. Attributes, as well as other features, are specified in a Document Type Definition (DTD).

## Document Type Declaration

It is possible to control the efficacy of information structured in an XML document through a construct known as a *Document Type Declaration*. A Document Type Declaration is an optional construct, but if present, it can be used to establish the validity of an XML document to insure that proper rules of formation have been followed. The rules are called the *schema*. A given XML document can have no schema, an internal schema, an external schema established for the specific document under consideration, or a public schema designed for a wide range of applications. Programs, known as *XML parsers*, are available to check the validity of an XML document against a specified schema.

This is important because XML is used for messaging between Internet services and not solely to service the "eyeball web."[67]

The existence of a Document Type Declaration is established through a DOCTYPE statement added to the prolog of an XML document. The usage of a DOCTYPE statement varies, depending upon the objective of the person designing the XML document. In its most simple form, the DOCTYPE statement names the root element and implicitly gives the name of the XML document, somewhat as follows:

```
<?xml version="1.0" ?>
<!DOCTYPE cars >
<cars>
    <manufacturer>Mercedes</manufacturer>
    <manufacturer>Porsche</manufacturer>
</cars>
```

In this example, the root element, namely **<cars>**, can be inferred from the document, but it is good practice to have it defined up front. This use of the DOCTYPE statement is optional.

A document type can be "public," as in the case of the definition of an HTML document in XML, as follows:

```
<?xml version="1.0" ?>
<!DOCTYPE html
    PUBLIC "-//w3c//DTD XHTML 1.0 Transitional//EN"
    SYSTEM"http://www.w3.org/TR/xhtnl1/DTD/xhtml
    1-transitional.dtd"
>
<html>
...
</html>
```

This use of the DOCTYPE statement is not optional. There are public document type declarations for a variety of applications, such as financial information exchange (OFX), mathematics (MathML), and wireless communications (WML).

---

[67] The eyeball web is a juicy way of saying that for most of us, the Internet and the World Wide Web are a means of finding information that we approach visually. It is quite another modality when one computer sends a message, ostensibly containing information, to another computer.

As far as a document type declaration for a particular XML document is concerned, such as one that we might develop, there are two options: internal or external. An internal type declaration is embedded in the XML document, as follows:

```
<?xml version="1.0" ?>
<!DOCTYPE cars [
```
(document type definition or schema for the *cars* root element)
```
]>
<cars>
    ...
</cars>
```

and in its external form as :

```
<?xml version="1.0" ?>
<!DOCTYPE cars SYSTEM "cars.dtd" >
<cars>
    ...
</cars>
```

where the SYSTEM option denotes a file indicator that is stored relative to the XML document file – perhaps in the same folder.

The schema rule structure, covered in subsequent sections, must apply to each element in an XML document.

## Character Data

With the preponderance of rules and the use of special characters, one could draw the conclusion that the use of XML for messaging would be severely limited in scope, flexibility, and practicality. That is definitely not the case. There is a construct in XML of the form:

```
<![CDATA[
```
(*You can place any textual data here*)
```
]]>
```

that permits a certain level of flexibility in the range of data that can be transmitted using XML-based messaging.

## Document Type Definition

A *Document Type Definition* (DTD) specifies the allowed structure of an XML document. A DTD is a simplified set of formation rules, whereas a schema can be viewed as a complicated set of rules. A document type declaration (DOCTYPE), covered previously, is not a DTD, although they are related to each other. The DOCYPE declaration indicates the *existence* of a definition, and the DTD *is* the definition. We are going to cover two forms of the former: element definition and attribute definition.

Recall the "book" example given previously:

```
<?xml version="1.0" ?>
<library>
    <library_name>Pleasure Books</ library_name>
    <book>
        <title>The DaVinci Code</title>
        <author>Dan Brown</author>
    </book>
    <book>
        <title>The Secret Servant</title>
        <author>Daniel Silva</author>
    </book>
</library>
```

A corresponding DTD, stored internally or externally, would be:

```
<!ELEMENT library (library_name, book+) >
<!ELEMENT library_name (#PCDATA) >
<!ELEMENT book (title, author) >
<!ELEMENT title (#PCDATA) >
<!ELEMENT author (#PCDATA) >
```

This definition specifies that **library** is the root element that should contain two child elements, namely **library_name** and **book,** in the given order. Moreover, the plus sign after the **book** element denotes that it can repeat. The definition also specifies that a **book** element should contain two child elements, namely **title** and **author,** in the given order, and each should consist of "parsed character data," indicated by the **#PCDATA** notation that indicates that the data part could consist of content and markup.[68] Data that

---

[68] Markup could be something like **&gt;**, for the "greater than" symbol, and **&lt;**, for the "less than" symbol. A nominal set of similar references are: **&apos;** for a single quotation mark, **&quot;** for a double quotation mark, and **&amp;** for the ampersand symbols.

is strictly textual could be denoted by CDATA. What this means is that with PCDATA, an XML parser should interpret it, and with CDATA, the XML parser should just take it as is.

## DTD Attributes

The reason for having an element in a data type definition is to establish a placeholder for storing content so that the data type definition can serve as a template for an XML document. The content can be extended through the use of an attribute. In the "book" example, an attribute could be a book's year of publication or its ISBN number.[69] The following script supplements the XML for the book example with an internal DTD that includes attributes for year, ISBN, and book category along with their corresponding elements:

```
<?xml version="1.0" ?>
<!DOCTYPE library [
    <!ELEMENT library (library_name, book+) >
    <!ELEMENT library_name (#PCDATA) >
    <!ELEMENT book (title, author) >
    <!ATTLIST book year CDATA #REQUIRED >
    <!ATTLIST book ISBN CDATA #IMPLIED >
    <!ATTLIST book category  (fiction | nonfiction) #REQUIRED >
    <!ELEMENT title (#PCDATA) >
    <!ELEMENT author (#PCDATA) >
]>
<library>
    <library_name>Pleasure Books</ library_name>
    <book year = "2003" ISBN = "0-385-50420-9" category = "fiction" >
        <title>The DaVinci Code</title>
        <author>Dan Brown</author>
    </book>
    <book year = "2007" ISBN = "0-399-15422-5" category = "fiction" >
        <title>The Secret Servant</title>
        <author>Daniel Silva</author>
    </book>
</library>
```

---

[69] ISBN is a book publisher's identification number that can consist of 10 or 13 digits. ISBN stands for International Standard Book Number.

Clearly, the DTD, just presented, is evidence that XML can get complicated very quickly. In this example, use of the terms **#REQUIRED** means that the attribute is required and **#IMPLIED** means that the attribute is optional. The statement:

```
<!ATTLIST book category  (fiction | nonfiction) #REQUIRED >
```

for example, means that the XML writer has no choice but to choose between fiction and nonfiction, as shown in the corresponding XML content.

## XML Schema

An *XML schema* is a way of defining an XML document based on the structure of the XML language, as compared to the DOCTYPE of definition that is an external form. Proponents of the XML schema methodology contend that it has advantages over a document type definition (DTD), because the validity of an XML document can be checked with an XML parser. XML schemas can be complicated and many people feel that the complexity is only beneficial when financial data are involved. The XML schema language, known as XMLSchema, is, in itself, defined in XML – analogous in a very general sense to the way you can define HTML in XML.

In an XML schema, the distinction between declarations and definitions is of primary concern. We declare elements and attributes and define data types, which can be simple or complex. We are going to refer to the expression in XML of information content as the *XML instance document*, and the XML specification of the structure and validity of the document as the *XML schema document*. A distinction is also made between being well-formed and being valid. When an instance document is well-formed, it adheres to syntactical and structural rules, primarily involving opening and closing tags and simple naming conventions. When an instance document is valid, on the other hand, it conforms to the specified data types of elements and how those elements relate to one another.. For straightforward messaging, the use of an XML schema may be more trouble than it is worth.

The following instance document (for example):

```
<?xml version="1.0" ?>
<theDocument>
Validity is everything.
</theDocument>
```

Can be validated by an XML parser with the following schema document:

```
<?xml version="1.0" ?>
<xsd:schema xmlns:xsd="http://www.w3.org/2001/XMLSchema">
```

```
<xsd:element name="theDocument" type ="xsd:string" />
</xsd:schema>
```

The instance document and the schema document must be separate files when using XML schemas. Here's how the schema system in XML works. Each XML schema processor, not to be confused with the XML parser, needs a description of the words used in the schema (such as **element** and **string**), and those words are stored as a namespace that also has a name. Remember, in the XML language, you have to define everything; nothing is built in. In this case, the namespace is named **xsd**. That is why each instance of one of the key words is prefixed with the namespace name, as in **xsd:element**. The prefix is needed because a schema could theoretically address more than one schema processor. The **XMLSchema** reference noted in the above schema script is that processor, and it defines the namespace **xsd**. When there is only one namespace, you actually don't need the prefix.

A more complicated instance document is given in Figure 6.10 and the corresponding schema document is given in Figure 6.11. As far as file naming is concerned, let the instance be called **schedule.xml** and the schema be called **schedule.xsd**. Also, assume they are both stored in the same folder to uncomplicate the naming. The schema document demonstrates several of the many options available with XML schemas: complex types, attributes, data types, and some structural elements.

---

```
<?xml version="1.0" ?>
<schedule
          xmlns:xsi="http://www.w3.org/2001/xmlschema-instance"
          xsi:noNamespaceSchemaLocation="schedule.xsd">
<course ID="CIS 2130">
          <course_title>Business Information Systems</course_title>
          <course_room>Cabot 213</course_room>
          <day_time>MW 1:00</day_time>
          <seats>30</seats>
          <enrollment>28</enrollment>
</course>
<course ID="CIS 3282">
          <course_title>Database Systems</course_title>
          <course_room>Cabot 130</course_room>
          <day_time>MW 2:30</day_time>
          <seats>25</seats>
          <enrollment>17</enrollment>
</course>
</schedule>
```

---

*Figure 6.10 XML Instance Document.*

```
<?xml version="1.0" ?>
<xsd:schema xmlns:xsd="http://www.w3.org/2001/XMLSchema ">
<xsd:element name="schedule">
    <xsd:complexType>
        <xsd:sequence maxOccurs="unbounded">
            <xsd:element name="course">
                <xsd:complexType>
                    <xsd:attribute="ID" type="xsd:string"/>
                    <xsd:sequence>
                        <xsd:element name="course_title"
                                        type="xsd:string"/>
                        <xsd:element name="course_room"
                                        type="xsd:string"/>
                        <xsd:element name="day_time"
                                        type="xsd:string"/>
                        <xsd:element name="seats"
                                        type="xsd:positiveInteger"/>
                        <xsd:element name="enrollment"
                                        type="xsd:integer"/>
                    </xsd:sequence>
                </xsd:complexType>
            </xsd:element>
        </xsd:sequence>
    </xsd:complexType>
</xsd:element>
</xsd:schema>
```

*Figure 6.11 XML Schema Document (for Figure 6.10).*

There is more to XML schemas, much more, but the examples give a flavor of what is involved with computer-to-computer messaging.

## Additional XML Features

There is a lot more to the XML language, such as a formal means of defining data types and stylistic structures for XML documents along with a whole host of operational facilities. If it would take one book to totally describe HTML, it would take two books to fully give the features in XML.

For a basic knowledge of service science, complete comprehension of XML is not needed – only an idea of what it is all about.

At this point, we have enough knowledge of service tools and techniques to proceed with Web Services, introduced in the next section. We are going to start with a specification of the XML grammar for a form of web messaging known as SOAP, which originally was an acronym for Simple Object Access Protocol.

# WEB SERVICES

A Web Service has been defined as any service that is available over the Internet, uses a standard XML messaging system, and is not dependant upon any one particular operating system.[70] This statement has the makings of something different from the "web service" that was presented earlier when discussing HTTP. Well, it is. Earlier, we described the human web wherein an end-user sends an informational request via HTTP to a web server, and the requested information is returned, also via HTTP, to the user's browser for visual display. In this section, we are going to cover the automated web, in which one computer sends information in the form of an XML document to another computer over the Internet, and the intended result is to initiate a service of some kind. The latter form is a well-defined web service model such that the name Web Service is a proper noun. It is important to mention that XML is used for things other than Web Services. It just so happens that they grew up together, so that they are naturally associated with one another.

## *Web Service Concepts*

There are two general approaches to using a Web Service. The first is to have one computer (*the sender*) send a simple message to a second computer (*the receiver*) and to have the receiver execute a procedure for the sender and return the result. The procedure is known as a *method* and the process is referred to as an XML-RPC, which stands for *XML-Remote Procedure Call*. A frequently used example to demonstrate the concept is the weather service application: a requester sends a zip code to the weather service program and the program (i.e., the method) returns the temperature. The initial request message can be written in XML as:

---

[70]See E. Cerami, *Web Services Essentials* ( Selected Reading), for much of the subject matter in this section.

```
<?xml version="1.0"?>
<weatherRPC>
   <weatherMethod>getTemperature</weatherMethod>
   <parameters>
        <zip_code>29909</zip_code>
   </ parameters >
</weatherRPC>
```

The example is conceptual and the message headers and other information are omitted. The response from the weather service would take the form:

```
<?xml version="1.0"?>
<weatherResponse>
   <parameters>
        <value><int>75</int></value>
   </parameters>
</weatherResponse>
```

XML-RPC can be implemented via an HTTP request/response or by embedding the informational content of the transaction in a SOAP message, which is the second approach.

SOAP is a protocol for exchanging information between computers where the structure of the information is represented in XML. Initially, SOAP was an acronym for Simple Object Access Protocol; things changed along the way and now SOAP stands for itself. The basic idea underlying SOAP is to make sure that programs running on two communicating computer platforms have the wherewithal to unambiguously understand each other. Accordingly, the XML element definitions from several namespaces need to be specified in a standard manner and also be accessible over the Internet. We are not going to include the definitions, per se, in the SOAP message, but instead, include a reference to the definitions, so that if things change, every message in the world does not have to change.

A simplex (i.e., one-way) message from a client to a server or from a server to a client is called a *SOAP message* and consists of a SOAP envelope in which is placed a message header and a message body. The optional header is intended to allow the inclusion of application-specific information, such as security and account numbers. The required message body contains the references and informational content of the SOAP message. Here is what the SOAP envelope looks like:[71]

```
<SOAP-ENV:Envelope
```

---

[71] This SOAP example is adapted from Cerami [2002] pp 51-52, including Figure 6.3.

```
xmlns:SOAP-ENV="http://schemas.xmlsoap.org/soap/
envelope/"
xmlns:xsi="http://www.w3.org/2001/XMLSchema-instance"
xmlns:xsd="http://www.w3.org/2001/XMLSchema">
    •
    •      ←----- The message body would go here
    •
</SOAP-ENV:Envelope>
```

and a sample message body is

```
<SOAP-ENV:Body>
    <ns1:getTemp
    xmlns:ns1="urn:xmethods-Temperature"
    SOAP-ENV:encodingStyle="http://schemas.xmlsoap.org/
    soap/encoding/">
        <zipcode xsi:type="xsd:string">29909</zipcode>
    </ns1:getTemp>
</SOAP-ENV:Body>
```

The complete application including the SOAP response is given in Figure 6.12. In fact, the method reference, namely **Temperature**, is determined during discovery and understood by the computer program receiving the SOAP message.

Again, comprehension is not required or expected. The scripts are exceedingly detailed, but one point is clear, even from this simple example. Once the structure of SOAP messaging is developed, the addition of the content is quite straightforward.

To sum up this section, SOAP messaging is straightforward. All one SOAP client has to do to send a message to another SOAP client is to put the content document into a predetermined SOAP message structure and send it through the Internet. It doesn't matter if the sender is a client or a server (in the generic sense) or the other way around. The sender and the receiver are both SOAP clients. The message itself is not important to the messaging process. It could be a request to have a method executed, or it could be a document, such as a financial report or a script representing a computer graphics procedure.

## Web Service Model

In order to request a service over the Internet, a person must go through a standard procedure. We covered this earlier. This is surprising considering all of the generality built into the World Wide Web. Figure 6.13 suggests the structure of Web Services architecture, which is another standard procedure.

There are three roles: the service provider, the service requester, and the service registry. The *service provider* makes a service available over the Internet. The *service requester* consumes a service by sending an XML message to the service provider over the Internet. The *service registry* is a centralized repository of information about services that are available, serving as a computer-oriented version of the traditional "yellow pages."

**SOAP Request**

```
<?xml version="1.0"?>
<SOAP-ENV:Envelope
    xmlns:SOAP-ENV="http://schemas.xmlsoap.org/soap/
    envelope/"
    xmlns:xsi="http://www.w3.org/2001/XMLSchema-instance"
    xmlns:xsd="http://www.w3.org/2001/XMLSchema">
    <SOAP-ENV:Body>
        <ns1:getTemp
        xmlns:ns1="urn:xmethods-Temperature"
        SOAP-ENV:encodingStyle="http://schemas.xmlsoap.org/
        soap/encoding/">
            <zipcode xsi:type="xsd:string">29909</zipcode>
        </ns1:getTemp>
    </SOAP-ENV:Body>
</SOAP-ENV:Envelope>
```

**SOAP Response**

```
<?xml version="1.0"?>
<SOAP-ENV:Envelope
    xmlns:SOAP-ENV="http://schemas.xmlsoap.org/soap/
    envelope/"
    xmlns:xsi="http://www.w3.org/2001/XMLSchema-instance"
    xmlns:xsd="http://www.w3.org/2001/XMLSchema">
    <SOAP-ENV:Body>
        <ns1:getTempResponse
        xmlns:ns1="urn:xmethods-Temperature"
        SOAP-ENV:encodingStyle="http://schemas.xmlsoap.org/
        soap/encoding/">
            <return xsi:type="xsd:float">75.0</return>
        </ns1:getTempResponse>
    </SOAP-ENV:Body>
</SOAP-ENV:Envelope>
```

*Figure 6.12 SOAP Request and Response.*

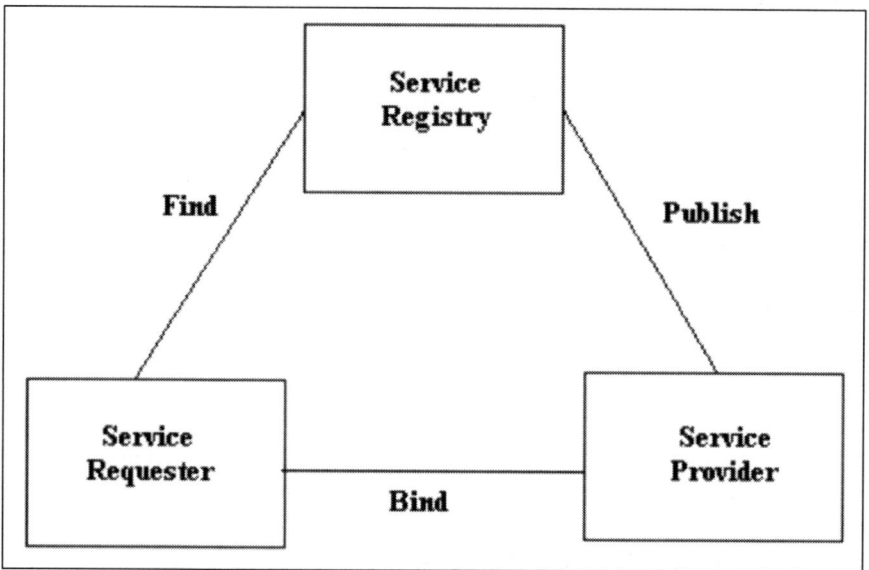

*Figure 6.13 Structure of the Web Service Model.*

Associated with the three roles are three activities. The service provider publishes available services in the service registry. The service requester finds out about services by accessing the service registry. The service requester invokes a service (called *bind*) by sending an XML message, referred to above, to the service provider. A familiar example of publish, find, and bind is an online book service. The prospective buyer consults the company's online catalog to find a suitable book. The buyer then finalizes the purchasing process by providing the requisite information, and the seller handles the billing and the physical transportation of the item purchased.

There is more to it, of course. When a service provider publishes service information, it must be described in a form that the service requester can understand. XML is used for this task by employing a document structure known a UDDI, which stands for *Universal Description, Discovery, and Integration.* When a service requester invokes a service, XML is again used in a form of descriptive language known as WSDL, which stands for *Web Services Description Language.*

## Web Services Description Language Operations

As its name implies, a WSDL document is a description of a web service. A service requester would use a WSDL to find a web service, establish a contract between itself and the service, and initiate the operation of that contract. In order to do the above operations, the WSDL document should specify six elements: definitions, data types, message types, port types, binding requirements, and a service element. The *definitions* section gives the name of the service and the namespaces involved. The *types* section specifies the data types used for communication between the service requester and the service provider. The *message* section describes each message (request or response) in the service contract. The *port type* section specifies the pattern of operation in the service being described. Operations are one-way, request-response, solicit-response, and notification (i.e., broadcast). The *binding* section describes how the service requester and the service provider will operate together, i.e., whether it is a remote procedure call or a transfer of a document. The *service* section gives the Internet location of the service.

Development of a WDSL document requires a lot of information, and that is where the UDDI comes in. It provides a template, among other things, for using a web service.

## Universal Description, Discovery, and Integration Operations

*Discovery* is the process of finding services that satisfy a particular need. A service registry is a database of services that facilitates discovery, and UDDI is an architecture for building that database. For an organization in the role of service provider, use of a registry can be a form of advertising and also a means of providing accessibility. For the service consumer, use of a service registry can provide information on the range of services available for a given need in addition to being a means of obtaining requirements for accessing a service.

At this stage in the development of service science, discovery is not completely automatic. Whereas, discovery can supply the name of a potential business partner or customer, a certain amount of person-to-person time is still required to establish a service level agreement.

UDDI architecture focuses on two major areas of user interaction: the UDDI data model and the methods for publishing entries to the registry. The latter set of methods refers to the application programming interface (API) for publishing and is not covered further in this book. The selected reading on this subject gives two good books on this subject that cover the programming aspects in some detail.

The UDDI data model focuses on three main categories of information: business entities, business service, and binding templates. The *business entity* element focuses on the actual business, such as name, description, address, and contact information. The *business services* element concentrates on information on a single business service. The *binding template* element gives information on how to connect to a particular service for information.

## Web Service Goal

The goal of Web Services was and still is the notion of having computers talk to each other to arrange for a service without human intervention. At this stage, the Internet community has done a commendable job of establishing the requisite technical infrastructure, but the process still requires client interaction at the service-requester end. The focus is currently on building a service-oriented architecture to support future developments.

Service-oriented architecture is covered in the next chapter.

# SUMMARY

Services are ubiquitous but require messages to communicate information between client and provider. A client and a provider can be tightly coupled, as when a patient is sitting in front of the doctor and they are having a give-and-take conversation, or loosely coupled, as when you send a request to someone via email and receive a response at some undetermined time in the future. In the former case, the client and provider are communicating in a *synchronous mode* without technology, and in the later case, they are communicating in an *asynchronous mode* with the use of technology.

The most profound aspect of service science is that a *service is a process*, as suggested by the following message pattern:

1.   A client sends a message to a service provider.

2.   The provider performs the required action and returns a message to the client.

The focus is on the data that is transmitted and not on the communications medium, which can take the form of a human interaction or a computer-based message. The context for the message can be embedded in the message or inherent in the way that the service provider is addressed. It is useful to recognize that we are operating at two levels: the service level and the message level. At the *service level*, the message entity that receives the message is the service provider, and in the case of a computer, it is regarded simply as the service. At the *message level*, there is some choreography involved with providing a service, as demonstrated by the above two-step interaction. In fact, a service may involve the interchange of several messages.

Many modern enterprises (i.e., business, government, education) provide computer support to internal users, clients, business partners, and other enterprise entities. The facilities are usually integrated into administrative, product development, supply chain, or customer relationship operations. Because those services, consisting of computer applications and associated procedures, are tried, tested, and dependable, it would be prudent to use them as building blocks for new enterprise applications. The concept that underlies service orientation is that it is simply more efficient and reliable to identify the bundled services and package them as reusable components than it would be to rewrite them. Bundled services could then be used by other services, so that information system applications could be developed more rapidly and enable the enterprise to be more responsive to external conditions.

In its most simple form, a message is a string of characters encoded using standardized coding methods commonly employed in computer and information technology. Messages have a uniform format consisting of a header and a body. The *header* primarily concerns addressing and includes the address of the sender and the receiver. In the request/reply message pattern, the return address is picked up from the message header for the response portion of the transaction. The *body* of the message contains the information content of the message and because it is intended only for the receiver, is not usually regarded during message transmission.

A service that takes place on the Internet and the World Wide Web is called a *web service*. A web service is a process in which the provider and client interact to produce a value; it is a pure service. The only difference between a web service and medical provisioning, for example, is that, in the former case, the client and provider are computer systems. The most pervasive web service computer application on the Internet is electronic mail, commonly known as email. The most widely used application on the World Wide Web is to find information. The major web technology tools and techniques are HTTP, HTML, and XML.

*HyperText Transfer Protocol* (HTTP) is a collection of rules and procedures for transferring messages between computers over the World Wide Web. Without HTTP, the web would not be the revolutionary phenomena that it is today.

It is possible to send a document from one computer to another and have that document displayed on the receiving end in a reasonable form without regard to the brand and model of computer, kind of software, time of day, and location. This feat is possible because of hypertext markup language (HTML).

Extensible Markup Language (XML) is a language and a standard for service messaging. Whereas HTML describes how a document will be rendered on the receiving end of a message, XML gives the semantics (or meaning) of a document.

A Web Service is any service that is available over the Internet, uses a standard XML messaging system, and is not dependant upon any one particular operating system.

# KEY TERMINOLOGY

The reader should be familiar with the following terms in the context in which they were used in the chapter.

Asynchronous mode
Bind
Body
Bot
Brokered topology
Description
Discovery
Document element
Document Type Declaration
Document Type Definition
Forward-only Server farm
Full duplex
Half duplex
Header
Hot link
HTML
HTTP
Hyperlink
Message pattern
Point-to-point
Schema
Service process
Service system
Simplex
SOAP
SOAP envelope
Synchronous mode
Tag
UDDI
URL
Web crawler
Web service
WSDL
XML

# A FEW GOOD QUESTIONS[72]

(1) A _____ is a collection of resources and economic entities, capable of engaging in or supporting one or more service events.

(2) A client and a provider can be _____, as when a patient is sitting in front of the doctor and they are having a give-and-take conversation, or _____, as when you send a request to someone via email and receive a response at some undetermined time in the future.

(3) A service is a _____.

(4) A _____ is a model of service communications that represents a single connection between one sender and one receiver.

(5) _____ refers to the manner in which messages are sent between messaging participants, and not necessarily to the communication techniques used to send them.

(6) URL stands for _____.

(7) HTTP stands for _____.

(8) HTML stands for _____.

(9) XML stands for _____.

(10) WSDL stands for _____.

(11) UDDI stands for _____.

---

[72] Answers: (1) service system; (2) tightly coupled, loosely coupled; (3) process; (4) message pattern; (5) message topology; (6) Uniform Resource Locator; (7) HyperText Transfer Protocol; (8) HyperText Markup Language; (9) eXtensible Markup Language; (10) Web Service Description Language; (11) Universal Description, Discovery, and Integration.

# SELECTED READING

Cerami, E., *Web Services Essentials*, Sebastopol, CA: O'Reilly Media, Inc., 2002.

Dykes, L. and E. Tittel, *XML for Dummies* (4$^{th}$ Edition), Hoboken, NJ: Wiley Publishing, Inc. 2005.

Gottschalk, K., Graham, S., Kreger, H., and J. Snell, "Introduction to Web services architecture," *IBM Systems Journal* (Vol. 41, No. 2), 2002, pp 170-177.

McGrath, M., *XML in Easy Steps*, New York: Barnes & Noble Books, 2003.

Musciano, C. and B. Kennedy, *HTML: The Definitive Guide*, Sebastopol, CA: O'Reilly Media, Inc., 1998.

Potts, S. and M. Kopack, *Web Services in 24 Hours*, Indianapolis: Sams Publishing, 2003.

Smith, J., *Inside Windows Communication Foundation*, Redmond, WA: Microsoft Press, 2007.

Spohrer, J., *Service Science, Management, and Engineering (SSME): State of the Art – service science*, IBM Nordic Service Science Summit, Helsinki, Finland, February 28, 2007.

Van Slyke, C. and F. Bélanger, *E-Business Technologies: Supporting the Net-Enhanced Organization*, New York: John Wiley and Sons, Inc., 2003.

Watt, A., *Teach Yourself XML in 10 Minutes*, Indianapolis: Sams Publishing, 2003.

Wikipedia, *HTTP*, www.wikipedia.org, 2007.

# 7

# Service Architecture

*Service architecture* is a collection of design patterns for constructing services from building blocks that can be shared between service systems. The methods have a technical flavor to them encompassing a set of principles for determining how the building blocks – referred to as *components* – should interact. Most business processes already incorporate a form of service architecture, since the principles are derived from ordinary common sense. For example, many accounting departments include component services, such as credit checking and invoicing, as does just-in-time manufacturing operations. When the objective is to align information services with business processes, however, the design gets more complicated and has given rise to a field of study known as *service-oriented architecture* (SOA). This chapter is ostensibly about SOA. The most interesting aspect of SOA is that the design principles apply as much, if not more, to enterprise processes as they do to computer processes.

## SERVICE ARCHITECTURE CONCEPTS

The basic idea behind service architecture is that you have a collection of components, representing business functions or computer applications, and you want to fit them together to make a business process or an information system. Figure 7.1 gives a generic view of a service architecture model. Each of the elements in the diagram is covered in this chapter.

As introduced in chapter five, components encapsulate services so that a service-oriented application or a business process is assimilated from multiple components that achieve the desired functionality by collectively orchestrating the operation of the needed services. The guiding principle behind service-oriented architecture is that once a component is established, it can be reused in other applications or business processes. Eventually, an organization runs out of components to build so that the synthesis of an application or a business process becomes a matter of piecing the components together – much like the manner in which an aircraft manufacturer or automobile company assembles relatively complicated products from off-the-shelf or specially-designed components, except that the objective is to construct service systems. There are two aspects to the idea of building functionality with components; the first is putting the components together, and the second is making the inherent services interact in such a way that a desired state of business process engineering (BPE) is achieved.

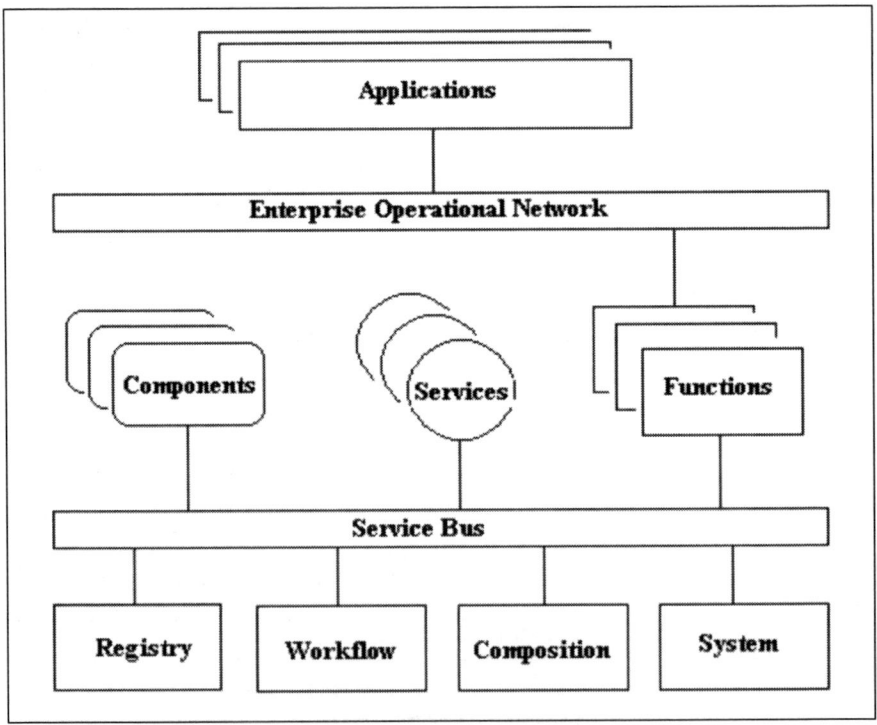

*Figure 7.1 Conceptual View of Service Architecture.*

## Solution Life Cycle

An effective solution sequence for any development project incorporates a set of well-defined steps, such as the following: requirements analysis, modeling, architectural design, detailed design, construction, and testing. In the modern view of development that incorporates service architecture, these steps are divided into two phases: the *preproduction phase*, wherein a set of packaged components are collected, and the *production phase*, consisting of assembly and deployment.

It is important to recognize that the term "production" in the context of service life cycle refers to the synthesis of a business process or the development of an information system, and not to the actual utilization of the process or system, as in everyday operations. So, in a sense, we are producing a solution and not running that solution at this stage of the life cycle. Once we have the wherewithal to assemble a solution from components and not have to develop those components from scratch, as they refer to it, then we can spend our resources making sure that the eventual solution to whatever problem we are dealing with actually satisfies business needs – and is developed in a reasonable time frame. This is where the term *agility* comes from. The management of an enterprise, for example, perceives that it needs an IT solution to an e-commerce opportunity, and the IT department can expeditiously deliver that solution.

Service-oriented architecture (SOA) has a side benefit with regard to systems development that is not entirely obvious. Modern information systems and business processes encompass mobile computing, Internet technology, and large-scale database dependencies are incredibly complex, often resulting in a focus on detailed *trees* rather than a more general *forest*. Service-oriented architecture invites us to look at the forest.

## On Demand

The term "on demand" seems to have navigated its way into the business literature in at least three ways. In the first instance, on demand refers to the access of information, such as from the World Wide Web or any other information repository, from wherever the end user may be and whenever the interaction takes place. In the second instance, on demand refers to access to computer application programs without specifically having to purchase them. Also known as *utility computing*, this form of on demand would allow end user to pay only for the use of software, rather than having to purchase it, as is typically the case with traditional office software. Finally, the third instance of on demand and the one in which we are interested refers to the techniques for the rapid development of business processes and computer information systems to support enterprise services.

The flexibility inherent in on demand services provides a payback for most enterprises that is greater than the value of the processes and applications for which the services were originally intended. Overall, on demand processes developed through service orientation can deliver innovation, flexibility, shorter time to market, and also serves as a vehicle for rethinking industry structures.[73] In fact, the business value of service architecture is perhaps best summarized by the following quotation from Cherbakov, Galambos, Harishankar, Kalyana, and Rackham:[74]

> What is described here is a business that is able to recognize change as it is occurring and react appropriately, ahead of the competition, and keep pace with demands of its customers, value-net partners, and employees alike. In trying to achieve this state, the business will need to leverage technology to the fullest. We call such a business an "on demand business." Fundamentally, becoming an on demand business is equivalent to achieving total business flexibility. Two important enablers contribute to the realization by an enterprise of this vision of on demand – componentization and service orientation.

Components are related to functions – or to be more specific, business components are related to business functions. In a real sense, therefore, service architecture refers to the deconstruction into components of an existing business system and subsequently its reconstruction into an operational network of cooperating and integrated elements needed for synthesizing responsive enterprise-wide systems.

## Components, Services, and Functions

It's all relatively straightforward: most components encapsulate one or more services; many complex services require more than one component; enterprise processes are constructed from components; and enterprise functions are an amalgamation of corresponding services. The notion of putting components together to achieve some enterprise function is called *composability*, and in order to do so, the methodology demands severe constraints on the manner in which the components are constructed and

---

[73] See Cherbakov, et al. (2005).
[74] Op. cit. p. 654.

packaged for reuse. Components must fit together in order to operate as intended; this requirement is known as *interoperability*.

### Service Orientation

Many people are going to say that dealing with a collection of interacting components is just going to increase the complexity of their everyday life. After all, they say, why not buy an application program or adopt an established business process and be done with it? On the other hand, there is something to be said for building systems out of packaged components. If a component fails, replace the entire assembly and let the customer – or should be say client – pay for it. After all, that perspective has some merit with products and is widely adopted. The point to remember is, "What's good for products is not necessarily good for services." Here are some of the reasons.

Because services are heterogeneous and involve client interaction, most service interactions are essentially different, so that the unrestricted use of packaged facilities does not automatically contribute to efficiency. With both products and services, features sell packaged facilities, so that if you obtain two related packages, there would normally be a duplication of functionality. In other words, organizations that produce packages, in the most general sense, include as many features as possible to optimize marketability. Most of us THINK products and DO services. Moreover, there is no guarantee that similar components in different packages operate – or interoperate – in exactly the same manner.

Another consideration is that in the area of professional, scientific, and technical services, the operant process is to construct a flexible system, perhaps for a client, in which components can be replaced on a demand basis to satisfy business conditions. In this instance, one would want each component to be designed as granular as possible with a well-defined interface.

## SERVICE-ORIENTED ARCHITECTURE OVERVIEW

Service-oriented architecture encompasses business-process modeling and software design. Flexibility and accessibility are the key ingredients in shifting from fixed resources to the notion of shared services, which is the cornerstone of service-oriented architecture. With service-oriented architecture, components are loosely coupled, which generally refers to a lack of inter-dependency between components, and can be referenced wherever they reside. An enterprise is service oriented if it can be properly viewed as a set of services connected to produce a specific result. Similarly, a computer application or information system is service oriented if it is constructed from interacting components running on the same platform or is accessible from different platforms via networking facilities.

## Incremental Development

Service orientation permits incremental development without having to make a serious commitment at every step of the way. At this stage in the worldwide development of information systems, vast resources are already in place. Business requirements can be satisfied by exposing key resources as services to be used in ongoing developmental activity. Clearly, the use of service technology, as introduced in chapter six, provides the basis for incremental development.

One of the key advantages of incremental development is that you don't have to bet the ship on every project. Large projects are difficult to initiate, cumbersome to sustain, and nearly impossible to terminate – even though business conditions sometimes change without notice. Reusable resources are the key to achieving a good return-on-investment.

## Business Models

Almost all enterprises have a business model.[75] We are interested in a business model based on components, so the place to start is with a definition of precisely what constitutes a business model. A *business model* is a conceptual description of the core elements constituting an organization along with a set of relationships between those elements that effectively determine the organization's value to customers, business partners, and shareholders.[76] A business model describes an organization's business and how it conducts that business. It usually consists of nine building blocks grouped into four categories,[77] as given in Figure 7.2. The elements are summarized as follows:

- The *business capabilities* describe the capabilities required to execute the organization's business.

- The *partner network* gives the business partners that complement the core capabilities.

---

[75] Actually, every enterprise has a business model, since the lack of a formal model is a convenient, but not necessarily satisfactory, means of operating and can properly be regarded as a business model.

[76] Three well-known business models are the razor-blade business model, the subscription business model, and the sell-make-deliver business model.

[77] See the referenced Wiki article on business models.

- The *value configuration* identifies the underlying basis for the organization from the following perspectives: the organization, the customers or clients, society, and other parties involved.

- The *value proposition* gives the value of the organization's services from the customer's or client's perspective.

- The *target audience* notes the collection of customers or clients to which the organization's services are directed.

- The *distribution channel* describes the means by which the customers or clients avail themselves of the organization's services.

- The *customer relationship* identified how the organization connects to the customer or client base.

- The *cost structure* describes how the organization views the finances involved with its operations, and the *revenue* gives the organization's income structure.

The entries are overlapping to some degree and repetitive. Taken together, however, they contribute to a description of how an organization does business.

There is another twist to business models. Each organization has a unique business model, even though there is some similarity between industries. In fact, IBM has identified component business models for sixty-nine industries.[78]

---

[78] Carter (2007) p. 29.

```
┌─────────────────────────────────────────┐
│                                           │
│            *Infrastructure*               │
│          Business capabilities            │
│            Partner network                │
│           Value configuration             │
│                                           │
│               *Offering*                  │
│                                           │
│            Value proposition              │
│                                           │
│               *Customers*                 │
│                                           │
│             Target customer               │
│           Distribution channel            │
│          Customer relationship            │
│                                           │
│                *Finances*                 │
│                                           │
│              Cost structure               │
│                 Revenue                   │
│                                           │
└─────────────────────────────────────────┘
```

*Figure 7.2  Business Model Building Blocks.*

## Componentization

One approach, perhaps the only approach, is to "break it all down," i.e., *deconstruction*, and then put it all back together, i.e., *reconstruction*, with a service-oriented perspective.  The business model component to be analyzed is the set of business capabilities.  We will call the set of capabilities *business competencies*, because some organizations typically do some things better than others, and some competencies are more fundamental to the value configuration of the organization than others.  When outsourcing is something an organization might want to do for logistical or financial reasons, non-core competencies are typically outsourced.

A generic set of business competencies are manage, design, build, test, buy, make, sell, and operate.  In addition, each competency can be viewed from each of three perspectives: direct, control, and execute.  Accordingly, each competency/perspective combination exists as a business component along with its corresponding activities.  It is the activities that require significant assets, such as people, technology, and organization.

Components are important because they support the associated business process.  Once identified, however, they can be reused to build other systems.  When used as building blocks for constructing systems, components are usually referred to as services, although we already know that a component may provide more that one service and sometimes a particular service requires more than one component, a process known as composition.

## Specialization

It has been hypothesized that in the near future, successful organizations will be "specialist" organizations because they will outsource support activities, and focus on core competencies. Even within core competencies, services can be shared between processes through the phenomena of computer networks and interoperability.

Recall the notion of a value net where components and their corresponding services can be sourced from business partners. The ability to quickly synthesize business systems from off-the-shelf components will imbue organizations with the capability of being more responsive to environmental, economic, and market conditions.

## Locality and Interoperability

Because of globalization, value nets, and the Internet, a required component for a business process can be available in a different location using an outsourced service infrastructure. If it is a computer-based business process, then the component could reside on a different platform at a remote location. In order to obtain the requisite service, the service requester would then have to send a web service message – typically using XML over the Internet– to receive a service. If it is a business process not directly involving computers, then the service could very well be supplied by a provider from a remote location .

# SERVICE-ORIENTED BUSINESS INFRASTRUCTURE

One of the motivating factors underlying service-oriented architecture is the simple fact that IT executives are now being held accountable for showing quantifiable results for the large IT investments that are usually incurred. The perspective espoused here is that IT managers are responsible for supplying technology-based business services, and that a service infrastructure synthesized from business components is fundamental to achieving business value from standard processes.

## Business Component Viewpoint

There are two perspectives that can be applied to component-based business models. The first is the traditional technology-centric IT perspective where components are independent of specific business processes. The second is the customer-centric perspective where the business services are the primary ingredient and the underlying technology is of secondary concern. This section is focused on the business benefits of component technology.

The identification of business components is a means of categorizing traditional enterprise activities to facilitate the identification of requisite business components. Any such set of components would necessarily be dependent upon a particular enterprise under study. To obtain an intuitive idea of what form the business components might take, we can go to the literature. In the service management issue of the *IBM Systems Journal*, Ernest and Nsavic[79] list eight generic components:

OPERATIONS. Day-to-day maintenance of production, delivery, support, and management of enterprise activities.

LEGAL/COMPLIANCE. Adherence to best practices based on standards, such as Sarbanes-Oxley and Gramm-Leach-Bliley Acts.

PRODUCT/SERVICE DEVELOPMENT. Use of knowledge management and business and information intelligence.

QUALITY ASSURANCE. Maintaining a comprehensive program of testing, release management, and change management.

CUSTOMER SATISFACTION. Supporting a customer focus through customer relationship management (CRM) systems.

COMMUNICATIONS. Making sure that an effective communications plan is in place between employees, customers, and business partners.

ACCOUNTING. Efficient business operations through financial and cost management.

ARCHITECTURE/CONSTRUCTION. Maintaining technology standards and relevant business organization for business operations.

Combining the generic business components with the traditional levels of management, namely strategic management, tactical management, and operational management, yields a component matrix representing operational functions at the highest level of the enterprise. Component-based business

---

[79] See Ernest and Nisavic (2007) p.389.

processes are incorporated into each of the elements in the component matrix so developed.

### Technology-Centric Viewpoint

From a technology perspective, we want to look into each of the areas, suggested in the preceding section, and identify the business requirements with regard to the technology needed to support that activity. This task is not so easy, since each enterprise is organized and operates differently. The basic idea is to develop a component map organized by business function to determine exactly what the requirements are.

The next step is to identify the services needed to support that activity, and we are well on our way to establishing a repository of existing and needed components.

# SERVICE DEVELOPMENT

On of the tenets of service science is that service providers can participate in a service experience by applying knowledge, skill, ingenuity, and experience,[80] without having to invest in the usual encumbrances of product development. In this section, we are going to cover *service development*, without having to necessarily develop each and every service resource. The subject matter primarily concerns "legacy systems," and the methodology applies to just about any kind of service an ordinary person can imagine.

### Phased Approach to Service Development

One of the better known approaches to service development involves five phases that constitute a set of best practices for achieving service innovation from existing services, as well as for the renovation of existing computer services:[81]

STRATEGY. Develop an overall service goal for the new service system and establish a set of steps to achieve that goal.

MODEL. Deconstruct the steps that comprise the existing system and identify those steps as service components.

---

[80] See the wiki reference to services.

[81] This list is adapted from the IBM publication on legacy systems renovation to SOA.

DEVELOP. Reconstruct the components for the new system and establish the choreography between the components so that the requisite business requirements are satisfied.

IMPLEMENT. Test, install, and monitor the execution of the new system.

MANAGE. Perform effective release, change, and risk management function to insure that the service system continues to meet stated goals.

The key elements in this process are the deconstruction and reconstruction of service components and the manage phases, because service architecture is continuously being adjusted to satisfy changing conditions.

## Legacy Systems

Many, if not most, information systems used in business, education, and government are known as *legacy systems* and continue to be the core of enterprise technology. For example, the "grunt" work underlying heavy duty data processing is performed behind the scenes, often during the wee hours of the night by mainframe computers. Linking these systems to modern Web services has been difficult, because they are difficult to change without running the risk of upsetting the applecart of good performance. The programs are written primarily in the COBOL programming language and precise specifications are not always available, adding another dimension to the problem.

Information systems that are cumbersome to change are referred to as being "brittle" and limit an enterprise's ability to respond to changing business requirements. On the other hand, legacy systems are serious assets to an organization and typically represent considerable investments. In many cases, organizations achieve a level of competitive advantage through the use of legacy systems. Legacy systems support day-to-day operations and incorporate the business logic inherent in all areas of the business model.

Service architecture purports to leverage legacy systems by unlocking the business functionality through loosely-coupled but well-structured service components abducted from legacy systems. The service components can then be choreographed to adapt or extend business processes to satisfy current needs. This can be achieved in two ways: leveraging or repurposing. With *leveraging*, the functions in legacy systems are exposed without rewriting the system. With *repurposing*, the programs are rewritten for the modern world with a modern language, such as Java, for use on servers designed for the Internet and the World Wide Web. Clearly, leveraging is the way to go with legacy systems, because of the risk involved with rewriting large programs and getting it right the first time.

## Exposing Functionality in Legacy Systems

Exposing business services by leveraging legacy systems is not a simple matter and it requires good strategic planning, time, and considerable resources. Typically, the work is outsourced to IT consulting companies, because a high level of expertise is required, but not otherwise needed to sustain enterprise operations.

Although the task is exceedingly complex, the idea is relatively simple: put a software wrapper around the legacy code and expose what you want to expose through well-defined interfaces. The conceptual software wrapper is known as an *adapter.*

Here's how it works. One component needs the services of another component, which may reside locally or be available over the Internet residing somewhere out in cyberspace. The needy component sends an XML message to the servicing component requesting a service of some kind. What this means is that the serving component does something and returns the result as an XML message to the requestor. The messages adhere to an agreed-upon format so that the programs can understand each other. (This is why we covered XML, SOAP, and all of those other topics in chapter six.)

The overall process is not much different than one person asking another person what time it is. The requestor issues the request in an agreed upon language in a well-defined format. The responder looks at a time resource and returns the time in the same language and in a related but different format. If another person asks for the time, the process is repeated. No additional questions asked.

There are some hidden components in the messaging scenario. The requestor needs information on who would know the time. So an internal registry of "people who know about time" is implicitly consulted before the initial message is sent by the requester to the responder. It's an example of the old adage, "George never knows what time it is, but he always knows where to buy ice." And so forth. With service architecture, a registry of components is needed to know which components to call upon when a particular service is needed. In the time example, one might look at the wrist of an associate to determine whether or not he or she has the wherewithal to give the time. Part of the registry process could very well involve a search process to determine which registry contains the needed information. Then, perhaps, the requestor might employ a local registry to hold pertinent information from non-local registries to facilitate subsequent operations.

There are security concerns with service architecture. For example, is the requestor authorized to receive the service it is requesting? This is also a topic we will cover later.

# SERVICE REFERENCE ARCHITECTURE

A certain amount of structure among components is required for the capabilities, mentioned above, to function together as a coherent whole. It is commonly known as the *SOA Reference Architecture*. The reference architecture is essentially a stack of functionality, implying that service messages flow upward and downward in the stack. Figure 7.3 gives a conceptual view of a hypothetical reference architecture.[82]

```
+---------------------------------+
|                                 |
|        User Interaction         |
|                                 |
|            Analysis             |
|                                 |
|          Orchestration          |
|                                 |
|       Services Management       |
|                                 |
|            Registry             |
|                                 |
|            Messaging            |
|                                 |
|            Services             |
|                                 |
+---------------------------------+
```

*Figure 7.3  Reference Architecture.*

## Loose Coupling

The basic principle of service architecture is that synthesis involves composition. A business process or a computer application is created by combining independent components that are loosely coupled. *Loose coupling*, in this instance, simply means that components – that is, the components providing the services – pass requests and data, in the form of messages, between each other in a standard manner without the need for underlying assumptions that would compromise component operational interdependence. Thus, a small change in the functioning of one component would not require a change to other components that rely on the changed

---

[82] The structure of the hypothetical reference architecture is adapted from the webMethods report (see selected reading, p. 5).

component. With component architecture of this sort, it is important to recognize that components normally relate to enterprise-level processes spanning people, systems, and information.

## Services

Services can be created or exposed. In the former case, an organization creates the business process or a computer application from scratch. In the latter case, an existing service is insulated with a logical container and its functionality is explicitly described so that other entities can use it. It's entirely possible that a service developed for another generation doesn't exactly fit in with what you are doing. In this instance, an adapter is needed to make whatever adjustments are necessary to use the service. It's like using your spouse as an adapter to your mother-in-law to arrange for babysitting service. In the world of computers, an *adapter* is a software module that permits access to a service through a standard messaging interface, usually created through the XML language.

Combining diverse services and exposing them as a single service is commonplace in everyday life. Consider, for example, a delivery service that combines three capabilities: dispatcher, driver, and accountant. The dispatcher interacts with the customers and makes the arrangements for the deliveries. The driver organizes his or her delivery route and makes the deliveries. The accountant records transactions, sends bills, and records payments. Yet, to the customer, there is only one service interface, which, in fact, is the point where the package is submitted for transportation. The delivery service has been composed from the three component services and the total process is called *composition*. Facilities, sometimes called *tools*, are needed to put references to components and corresponding services in the registry so that system designers can find them. All of this points to why the subject of web services is so important. Web services with its associated XML, SOAP, UDDI, and WSDL facilities, provide a convenient means of establishing a reference architecture.

## Messaging

The messaging layer of the service reference architecture provides the means for the components to interact and emphasize the need for in-between functionality to provide the requisite level of independence required by SOA. Consider, for example, an investment firm that supports a database of up-to-the-second stock prices. An investment advisor with a client on the line would like the latest price of AT&T stock. So he or she enters the stock exchange code for AT&T, namely 'T', and presses a key on the advisor's workstation. In a flash, the current stock price is returned. Some in-between hardware and software, known as *middleware*, is required to make it all happen. Clearly, many other services within the investment firm would also utilize the same stock price service. It's a simple example but gives evidence that the component-based approach to system development has some definite merit.

A messaging service would normally use *asynchronous messaging*, which means that the requestor sends the message to the service and the result is returned as soon as possible. While the person may be waiting for a response operating in a synchronous mode, the underlying hardware and software goes along its merry way sending messages back and forth asynchronously. Because of the great difference in processing speeds of humans and computers, it appears as though the computer is sitting there waiting for a request and responds immediately. In reality, that request may be put on a queue and processed in order of arrival, recognizing that different methods for queue management may be used.

## Registry

The concept of a registry was introduced previously in the context of legacy systems and web services. With web services, the registry is a general facility for storing service information that can be retrieved through XML messaging. It's more complicated but that's the idea. With service architecture, as in the present context, the registry is a repository for information on components, intended for persons synthesizing a composite service, and additionally contains tools to assist in achieving that synthesis. *The registry is a data base of components and the services they supply.*

The registry should also contain facilities for convenient search, the import and export of entries, and change management. In the latter instance, it is necessary for users to be informed of updates that might affect their performance.

The registry should additionally reflect business policy as it refers to distribution, security, and ownership.

## Architecture Services Management

In the present context, services management refers to the operation and management control over business processes constructed with a service orientation. The efficacy of service operations is always of concern as it relates to service-level agreements as they relate to performance and quality of service. In the former case, performance encompasses the availability and reliability of individual services. In the latter case, quality of service refers to the statistical analysis of specific service events.

Management control reflects governance concepts as they apply to the operations mission, previously mentioned. Governance should reflect the fact that service architecture is a methodology for using services to construct services and has two major focuses: (1) The creation of processes, operating in the form of services, to support both IT-enabled and non-IT-enabled business activities; and (2) The control and support of the business services through a formal process for managing services. Accordingly, effective governance demands that an infrastructure, such as the one suggested by Figure 7.4, be in place for handling the following activities:

- *Changing* – introduces new/change services
- *Operating* – executes day-to-day activities
- *Supporting* – resolves incidents and problems
- *Optimizing* – enhances cost, performance, capacity, and availability services

To summarize, governance provides support for empowering people to do what they do in line with organizational objectives.

## Orchestration

*Orchestration* refers to the dynamic linking of services together to achieve a business purpose. The business processes are layered on top of the services, so in a sense, the services are anchored into the processes. In IT-enabled processes, the business process is a script written in a "business process execution language" that successively calls the needed components in order to invoke the services constituting the business function. This combinatory operation was earlier referred to as composition and can be conceptualized as the workflow of services. In a non-IT enabled process, the composition is achieved through management directed policies, procedures, and business rules.

Actually, the term "orchestration" has two meanings in the context of service science. Let's take a computer application as an example. The first meaning has to do with setting up the structure as a controlling module that successively invokes services to achieve a business objective. The components do not have some form of inherent stickiness that enables operational affinity among loosely-coupled components in a meaningful order. That is where the business process execution language (BPEL), referred to just above, comes in. The application designer has to set up the service chain beforehand.

This is where the operational structure in Figure 7.1 comes into play. The service bus effectively connects the registry, workflow, composition, and the underlying system (called the *platform*) as pieces that do the work to construct function from components viewed as services.

The second meaning of the term "orchestration" refers to the actual running of the application. The BPEL script is actually executed by as operational entity, intermediate data is stored in an operational database (not shown), and the business result is achieved.

For non-IT enabled processes, orchestration is established and controlled by an operational manager.

### Analysis

One of the facets of the service domain is that service quality is directly related to client interaction and involvement. This requires constant tweaking, otherwise known as continuous improvement (i.e., *kaizen* in operations management). Business performance is constantly monitored – there is nothing new about this. With service systems, however, the raw operational data is frequently embedded deep down in independently constructed loosely-coupled components. Getting this data out for analysis is a task that should be addressed at the design level.

### User Interaction

On the surface, the end-user interface development model seems simple. All that needs to be done is to construct a prototype, test it, improve it, and then have the end-user group sign off on it. With service-oriented architecture, however, the *user interaction* is with a business process, which is a notch up from what normally is construed as the end-user interface. The term "user," therefore, refers to the user of a service, and not necessarily to the user of an application. As in the restaurant example, the user of a service doesn't have to be the customer.

The user of a service can be another service, which leads to the notion of a service architecture in which components can be assembled without the use of special adapters.

## SERVICE ARCHITECTURE PRINCIPLES

The use of design principles is paramount to the construction of a successful service project. Otherwise, service systems development is another "random walk down Wall Street." Here is a set of service architecture principles, abstracted from several sources – primarily the Wiki article on Service-Oriented Architecture:

- Service Abstraction
- Service Encapsulation
- Service Loose Coupling
- Service Contract
- Service Reusability
- Service Composability
- Service Autonomy
- Service Discoverability

The principles are used in the next chapter, when developing a model for component interaction. Most of the principles have been addressed implicitly is preceding sections, but it is necessary to have them specifically identified for descriptive purposes.

## Service Abstraction

The key benefit of service abstraction is that "inside" information about a component is effectively hidden from the outside so that component can be used by other diverse services. This principle is sometimes referred to as information hiding. Often, internal operational details are superfluous to a referencing service where only a result is needed. Take the credit checking service as an example. An outside user of that service is usually only interested in the credit worthiness of a subject and not in the procedures and file processes necessary to ascertain that rating. In fact, operational details may change without the requester knowing or caring about them. The concept of abstraction applies to other organizational functions and computer modules, as well.

## Service Encapsulation

Service encapsulation enables a service – often bundled as part of a larger operational entity – to be referenced via an adapter to preserve and take advantage of previously developed functionality. As with the preceding principle, encapsulation may apply to organizational as well as informational components.

## Service Loose Coupling

This principle simply demands that components are not implicitly dependent upon one another, such that use by a non-coupled component is prohibited. Another way of expressing the concept of loose-coupling is one component does not require that another component be in a particular state at the time of invocation.

## Service Contract

The concept of a service contract reflects that it is necessary that a complete specification be made of the precise services provided by a service component and exactly how those services are to be addressed. A service contract describes how two components are to interact. With Web services, the contract refers to a WSDL (Web Services Definition Language) definition and a specification of the XML schema definition of precisely how messages between a requester and the repository be formatted.

## Service Reusability

Service reusability simply refers to the practice of designing a component so that it can be used in more than one place. In general, the intention is to provide services that can be used by more than one business process.

## Service Composability

Service composability refers to the combining of services to form composite services. This practice implicitly imposes a restriction on the component services that they adhere to the specifications in the service contract, implying that service design – although simple to understand – is not necessary easy to achieve.

Service composition is usually performed to synthesize a business process.

## Service Autonomy

Service autonomy is conceptually modeled after the human nervous system and refers to a component's capability to self-govern its own operational behavior. Autonomy reduces the complexity of business processes composed from self-regulating components. Autonomy allows a business process to provide a higher level of productivity by being able to manage itself. This is a tricky principle, because the implication is that a component just operates on its own as some artificial intelligence robot. For most services, this principle simply means that a service invoked through some form of "service bus" takes its input parameters and performs its functions, as specified in its service contract, without requesting additional input or operating instructions.

## Service Discoverability

Service discoverability is a complex arrangement of being describable, via the service contract, and being accessible via a registry and a description language. Essentially, this means that the description of a service, found through a search process, additionally provides information on how to use a service.

# SERVICE ARCHITECTURE STRUCTURE AND OPERATION

A business process is composed of one or more business services frequently implemented through information and communications technology (ICT). Krafzig, Banke, and Slama[83] state the modern dependence on ICT in the following way. "... enterprises heavily depend on the IT backbone, which is responsible for running almost all processes of modern enterprises, be they related to manufacturing, distribution, sales, customer management, accounting, or any other type of business process." This section introduces the concept of enterprise systems and then presents definitive information on the structure and operation of service architecture in an enterprise environment.

## Enterprise Systems

An enterprise system cuts across the total organization and encompasses inter-departmental dependencies and relationships with suppliers and business partners. Accordingly, the enterprise software should be tightly coupled with the organization, but not with itself, based on the component model. This reflects the agility and incremental change that we referred to earlier. We require a structure that promotes loose coupling through messaging and platform interoperability.

## Service Architecture Structure

The key structural elements in a service system are the services, a service repository, the service broker, the service bus, the service manager, and the interface elements. The interface elements can be to end users or to application programs.

From a structural viewpoint, the *service* provides business logic and consists of an implementation and a service contract. The *service repository*,

---

[83] See their book in the selected readings, p.1.

operating as a virtual library, exists as a place to store service information and how to retrieve that information. The service repository certainly has a computer flavor to it, but need not be the case. Many service firms have manual lists of the services they offer. In the computer version of a service repository, however, the storage facility could be accessed manually during development and dynamically during the execution of a component. The *service broker* connects services together by accessing the service repository for information about services and providing the linkage to connect components. The *service bus* is the nerve center in an enterprise system and is covered separately, as is the service manager, which is the mechanism by which enterprise processes are constructed. The interface elements are the input and output to the system.

The term "interface" normally implies an end-user interface with which most persons are familiar. In the case of enterprise systems, however, an interface can be to another computer application, a database, or a legacy system.

## Enterprise Service Bus

An *enterprise service bus* (ESB) is a collection of ICT facilities for routing messages between services, or more specifically between components. The bus metaphor is apt in this case. The message gets on, goes to its destination, and gets off. The metaphor ends there, because there are different kinds of busses and unique things happen on different busses.

The most straightforward kind of service bus is a high-speed data link between services, as alluded to earlier in the stock broker example. The stock broker needs the current price of a stock for an ongoing transaction. The stock symbol is entered into a workstation and a button is pressed. In a fraction of a second, the current price is returned by a service connected to the other end of the service bus. The service bus in this instance, is a combination of hardware and software often referred to as middleware. In this model of bus, the service bus could also be a specially constructed data link between business partners or between organizational units, termed electronic data interchange (EDI).

The most general form of ESB, however, uses the Internet with all of its inherent requirements for interoperability. In this instance, a message, perhaps requesting a service, may go through a necessary protocol conversion in its route from sender to receiver. Another possible function performed by an ESB is *context mediation*, which refers to a change in value based on contextual differences. An example would be the change of a price from Yen to Dollars during message processing.

Another related topic is *web based intermediary*, or WBI for short. A WBI is a program that runs in concert with a client's browser and acts as a form of software assistant, filtering and preparing information to satisfy particular needs.

## Service Manager

The most prevalent use of service architecture is to construct computer applications. The service manger ties everything together and runs the show. Clearly, this is an operational function but a structural component is needed to do it. In a sense, the service manager is the "main program" of an application. The service manager could be a specially written component in an enterprise system, or it could be a vendor-supplied package that successively calls upon required services.

## Service Architecture Operation

An enterprise system is sometimes referred to as an "end to end" operation that represents a business process. Another means of conceptualizing an enterprise system is that it is controlled process flow. As covered above, the service manager controls the process flow through a process called *orchestration*. The conductor of an orchestra controls the activity of a set of musicians through minute actions termed orchestration. The same concept can be applied to the execution of an enterprise system.

Orchestration is different than choreography. Choreography refers to what a collection of services can do, and orchestration refers to precisely when and how they actually they do it.

A business process can be scripted in a language, such as BPEL, written in a computer language, such as Java, or monitored using a system, such as JBoss. Business Process Execution Language (BPEL) is an XML-based scripting language for orchestrating service applications.[84]

# SUMMARY

*Service architecture* is a collection of design patterns for constructing services from building blocks that can be shared between service systems. The basic idea behind service architecture is that you have a collection of components, representing business functions or computer applications, and you want to fit them together to make a business process or an information system.

---

[84] For a good reference to BPEL, see Margolis (2007).

Components encapsulate services so that a service-oriented application or a business process is assimilated from multiple components that achieve the desired functionality by collectively orchestrating the operation of the needed services. The guiding principle behind service-oriented architecture is that once a component is established, it can be reused in other applications or business processes. Eventually, an organization runs out of components to build so that the synthesis of an application or a business process becomes a matter of piecing the components together.

An effective solution sequence for any development project incorporates a set of well-defined steps, such as the following: requirements analysis, modeling, architectural design, detailed design, construction, and testing.

The term "on demand" seems to have navigated its way into the business literature in at least three ways. In the first instance, on demand refers to the access of information, such as from the World Wide Web or any other information repository, from wherever the end user may be and whenever the interaction takes place. In the second instance, on demand refers to access to computer application programs without specifically having to purchase them. Also known as *utility computing*, this form of on demand would allow end users to pay only for the use of software, rather than having to purchase it, as is typically the case with traditional office software. Finally, the third instance of on demand and the one in which we are interested refers to the techniques for the rapid development of business processes and computer information systems to support enterprise services.

It's all relatively straightforward: most components encapsulate one or more services; many complex services require more than one component; enterprise processes are constructed from components; and enterprise functions are an amalgamation of corresponding services. The notion of putting components together to achieve some enterprise function is called *composability*, and in order to do so, the methodology demands severe constraints on the manner in which the components are constructed and packaged for reuse. Components must fit together in order to operate as intended; this requirement is known as *interoperability*.

An enterprise is service oriented if it can be properly viewed as a set of services connected to produce a specific result. Similarly, a computer application or information system is service oriented if it is constructed from interacting components running on the same platform or is accessible from different platforms via networking facilities.

There are two perspectives that can be applied to component-based business models. The first is the traditional technology-centric IT perspective where components are independent of specific business processes. The second is the customer-centric perspective where the business services are the primary ingredient and the underlying technology is of secondary concern.

Service architecture purports to leverage legacy systems by unlocking the business functionality through loosely-coupled but well-structured service components abducted from legacy systems. The service components can then be choreographed to adapt or extend business processes to satisfy current needs. This can be achieved in two ways: leveraging or repurposing. With *leveraging*, the functions in legacy systems are exposed without rewriting the system. With *repurposing*, the programs are rewritten for the modern world with a modern language, such as Java, for use on servers designed for the Internet and the World Wide Web. Clearly, leveraging is the way to go with legacy systems, because of the risk involved with rewriting large programs and getting it right the first time.

A certain amount of structure among components is required for the capabilities, mentioned above, to function together as a coherent whole. It is commonly known as the *SOA Reference Architecture.*

The use of design principles is paramount to the construction of a successful service project. A set of service architecture principles includes the following elements: service abstraction, service encapsulation, service loose coupling, service contract, service reusability, service composability, service autonomy, and service discoverability.

An enterprise system cuts across the total organization and encompasses inter-departmental dependencies and relationships with suppliers and business partners. Accordingly, the enterprise software should be tightly coupled with the organization, but not with itself, based on the component model. The key structural elements in a service system are the services, a service repository, the service broker, the service bus, the service manager, and the interface elements. The interface elements can be to end users or to application programs. An *enterprise service bus* (ESB) is a collection of ICT facilities for routing messages between services, or more specifically between components.

An enterprise system is sometimes referred to as an "end to end" operation that represents a business process. As covered above, the service manager controls the process flow through a process called *orchestration*. Orchestration is different than choreography. Choreography refers to what a collection of services can do, and orchestration refers to precisely when and how they actually they do it.

# KEY TERMINOLOGY

The reader should be familiar with the following terms in the context in which they were used in the chapter.

Abstraction
Analysis
Autonomy
Choreography
Component
Composability
Develop
Discoverability
Encapsulation
Implement
Interoperability
Legacy system
Loose coupling
Manage
Message
Model
On Demand
Orchestration
Preproduction phase
Production phase
Registry
Reusability
Service
Service architecture
Service bus
Service contract
Services management
SOA reference architecture
Solution lifecycle
Strategy
User interface
Utility computing

# A FEW GOOD QUESTIONS[85]

1) _____ is a collection of design patterns for constructing services from building blocks that can be shared between service systems.

2) In the modern view of development that incorporates service architecture, the steps are divided into two phases: the _____ _____, wherein a set of packaged components are collected, and the _____ _____, consisting of assembly and deployment.

3) _____ computing is a form on demand service.

4) The concept of putting components together to achieve some enterprise function is called _____.

5) A _____ _____ is a conceptual description of the core elements constituting an organization along with a set of relationships between those elements that effectively determine the organization's value to customers, business partners, and shareholders.

6) _____ _____ means that components pass requests and data, in the form of messages, between each other in a standard manner without the need for underlying assumptions that would compromise component operational interdependence.

7) _____ refers to the dynamic linking of services together to achieve a business purpose.

8) Service _____ is conceptually modeled after the human nervous system and refers to a component's capability to self-govern its own operational behavior.

9) Service _____ is complex arrangement of being describable, via the service contract, and being accessible via a registry and a description language.

10) _____ refers to what a collection of services can do, and _____ _____ refers to precisely when and how they actually they do it.

---

[85] Answers: (1) Service architecture; (2) preproduction phase, production phase; (3) utility; (4) composability; (5) business model; (6) loose coupling; (7) orchestration; (8) autonomy; (9) discoverability; (10) choreography, orchestration.

# SELECTED READING

Carter, S., The *New Language of Business*, Upper Saddle River, NJ: IBM Press, 2007.

Cherbakov, L., Galambos, G., Harishankar, R., Kalyana, S., and G. Rackham, "Impact of service orientation at the business level," *IBM Systems Journal*, Vol. 44, No. 4, 2005, pp. 653-668.

Erl, T., *Service-Oriented Architecture: A Field Guide to Integrating XML and Web Services*, Upper Saddle River, NJ: Prentice Hall, 2004.

Erl, T., *SOA: Principles of Service Design*, Upper Saddle River, NJ: Prentice Hall, 2008.

Ernest, M. and J.M. Nisavic, "Adding value to the IT organization with the Component Business Model, *IBM Systems Journal*, Vol. 46, No. 3, 2007, provider.387-403.

Hagel, J. and J.S. Brown, *The Only Sustainable Edge*, Boston: Harvard Business School Press, 2007.

Hurwitz, J., Bloor, R., Baroudi, C., and M. Kaufman, *Service Oriented Architecture for Dummies*, Hoboken, NJ: Wiley Publishing, Inc., 2007.

IBM Corporation, *Extend the value of your core business systems: Transforming legacy applications into an SOA framework*, Form G507-1950-00, September 2006.

Krafzig, D., Banke, K., and D. Slama, *Enterprise SOA: Service-Oriented Architecture Best Practices*, Upper Saddle River, NJ: Prentice Hall, 2005.

Margolis, B. with J. Sharpe, *SOA for the Business Developer: Concepts, BPEL, and SCA*, Lewisville, TX: 2007.

webMethods, *SOA Reference Architecture: Defining the Key Elements of a Successful SOA Technology Framework*, www.webMethods.com, 2006.

Wikipedia, *Business Models*, www.wikipedia.com, 2008

Wikipedia, *Services*, www.wikipedia.com, 2008

Woods, D. and T. Mattern, *Enterprise SOA: Designing IT for Business Innovation*, Sebastopol, CA: O'Reilly Media Inc., 2006.

# 8

# Service Business

A thriving flexible service economy has emerged through globalization and digitization, and as a direct result, the modern enterprise has a dynamically changing boundary based on a portfolio of services obtained through make, buy, or rent decisions. The decisions are taken, of course, through an analysis of transaction costs.[86] This dynamism has been fueled by service innovation, service marketing, and Internet-based business models. In the latter case, inexpensive and ubiquitous computing and interoperability have practically eliminated geographic barriers to growth and flexibility. This chapter describes a business model based on services.

## SERVICE BUSINESS CONCEPTS

Several important factors have contributed to the new business model based on services. The complexity of the modern work environment is perhaps the key factor as well as the changing demands of a networked

---

[86] A *transaction cost* is defined as the overall cost of economic exchange between two economic entities and includes finding, sustaining, and consuming goods and services from suppliers, business partners, and in-house sources.

economy. The increased level of worldwide incomes has added to the desire for enhanced business and social services. The dependence on information and communications technology (ICT) has been an enabler of the complexity and growth of services by facilitating the connection between suppliers and consumers of services.

## Business Model

A *business model* is a representation of a business emphasizing its purpose, strategies, organization and operational practices, and capabilities. It typically covers the following: core capabilities, partner network, value proposition, customer base, distribution methods, cost structure, and revenue base.[87] One of the functions of a business's organizational and operational structures is to translate the business model into an objective reality.

The point of view taken here is that an operational service model is a business model.

## Strategy and Mission

A *strategy* has been defined as "A long term plan of action designed to achieve a particular goal," and *governance* as "The set of processes, customs, policies, laws, and institutions affecting the way an endeavor is directed, administered, or controlled."[88] The two subjects command our attention, because much of the economy and workforce are engaged in services; but, as we have alluded to before, we seem to know the least about what we do the most.

The basic tenet underlying strategy is that a principal entity desires to accomplish something worthwhile called a *mission*. A mission is required so the entity, be it a business, firm, government agency, educational unit, or person, knows where it is going, and a strategy is needed so it knows how to get there. The mission is a service participant's goal, and the strategy is the roadmap for achieving that goal. A *strategy* is a plan of action.

## Service Ecosystem Characteristics

Before the revolution in ICT services, the exchange of information was a supporting element in most aspects of economic activity. Through

---

[87] For a complete list, see the Wiki article on business models.
[88] Adapted from the Wikipedia articles on strategy and corporate governance.

advanced technology, information is now an important component in the value proposition of most services.

The modern enterprise can now exploit informational resources on a demand basis from remote locations and without necessarily owning them. Moreover, the facilities necessary to sustain those resources may be shared, creating innovative opportunities for service provisioning.

Through web sites, mobile computing, and kiosks, self-service channels are currently available to support informational interchange. Business functions, such as billing, payments, ordering and order processing, reservations, online service support, and information management, are currently available without regard to time or distance.

Through innovation and entrepreneurship, new business opportunities are available on an on-demand basis, frequently constructed from existing services.

## Strategic Assets

A *strategic asset* is a resource that provides the basis for core competencies, economic benefit, and competitive advantage, thereby enabling a service business to provide distinctive service in the marketplace. Because services are labor intensive, investments in people, processes, knowledge, and infrastructure are directly analogous to investments in resources for production and distribution in capital intensive businesses.

Strategic assets permit a service enterprise to achieve a competitive advantage through service differentiation, cost advantage, and superior customer response. *Service differentiation* involves providing a high degree of uniqueness in the service experience and also in the quality of service provided. *Cost advantage* refers to efficiency in the use of facilities, as in an airline terminal, and with 24/7 operations to maximize the use of infrastructure. *Customer response* involves flexible, reliable, and timely solutions to customer requirements.

## Service Context

A *service context* supports the efficacy of service provisioning. The development of a service context involves the asking of tough questions to examine the strategic goal and objectives of a service organization in order to identify and establish a service portfolio. Here are some questions a service organization might want to [89]ask of itself:

---

[89] Adapted from ITIL, p.9.

- What services should we offer?

- To whom should the services be offered?

- How do we achieve competitive advantage?

- What is our customer's value proposition?

- How do we establish value for our stakeholders?

- How do we define service quality?

- How do we allocate strategic assets to our service portfolios?

- What are the bottlenecks to growth and effective service provisioning (i.e., constraint management)?

The questions apply in differing degrees to whether services are provisioned for one organization (or department), one of more units within the same parent organization, or to units in different organizations. Moreover, the services apply within the following contexts: do them yourself, another business entity helps you do them, and have another business entity do them for you.

### Service Perspective

Every reasonable business model demands a context and the one that we present in this chapter is no exception. Our service model is based on a service management concept for providing value to customers in the form of capabilities that translate resources into valuable services.

The objective of service provisioning – regardless of whether the service involves people processing, possession processing, or information processing – is to provide value to customers through an intrinsic knowledge of customer needs obtained by preparation, analysis, usage patterns, and the application of best practices. Within this perspective, a *service* may be alternately defined as a means of delivering value to customers by facilitating outcomes customers want to achieve without the ownership of specific costs and risks.[90]

## SERVICE SYSTEMS THINKING

The objective of a service business is to assist in making resources available to the client as services, and in the process, creating value for both provider and client. This is a worthwhile objective, to be sure, but some basic questions must first be answered. Who are the client and the provider? What are the resources? What geopolitical forces are involved? Does the nature of the service itself play

---

[90] See Clark (2007), p.5.

an important role in the process of value creation? And, so forth. Clearly, the questions are primarily rhetorical. However, we can go a long way by considering the next question. Are we service creationists or are we service evolutionists? The answer to this particular question is important, because it determines precisely how we approach the subject of service provisioning. Before we get going with the discussion of the subject, one of the questions can be answered right off the top, and it has to do with resources. For any organization we are going to consider, the key resources are people, organization, infrastructure, technology, and capital.

## Service Factors

Three factors determine the need for services and the realization of those services. They are: value, flexibility and control, and risk. With regard to the value factor, it is not just value, per se, but value versus cost. When costs are reduced through internal or external outsourcing, for example, there is a normal concern over whether the value to the client is the same as or greater than before the outsourcing. Using resources and capability as inputs to a service, is the resulting value to the client commensurate with the cost? Similarly, when internal or external outsourcing is implemented, there is concern over operational flexibility and management control. Some organizations have experienced the "tail wagging the dog" syndrome and have had to bring major services, such as IT outsourcing, back into the parent organization. It is very difficult to modify strong service level agreements, so the parent organization is effectively constrained by the very services that were supposed to provide them with business agility. Also, successful outsourcing, in some instances, has effectively been jeopardized through mergers and acquisition, whereby competing services have been assimilated into a parent organization thereby comprising the original benefits. Lastly, there is risk inherent in relying on services, even though there is a customary risk to be expected in everyday affairs. The uncertainty in the application of service level agreements works contrary to the expectation on the part of clients to receive a positive effect with the utilization of assets. To inject a bit of reality into the analysis, there is always the headache factor. The possibility always exists that outsourcing or calling in a consultant, is a means of getting rid of an organizational or operational headache – regardless of the cost; and similarly, living with outsourcing may be too much for some organizations to handle.

## Service Creationism

In most views of service theory, there would appear to be service creationist forces at work. Through some unknown process, an enterprise comes to life and ostensibly needs service of some kind.[91] A service organization enters the scene and identifies certain processes associated with the enterprise that it can use to make a profit. It's clear that the target enterprise is the service client, and the service organization is the service provider. The activity on the part of the provider that identifies candidate processes for the proposed benefit of the client is sometimes called service innovation. Usually, service innovation amounts to very little more than an elementary form of observational research.[92] In general, however, the tasks involved with creating and sustaining a service business usually constitute a rational process. The provider may possess superior capability, as is commonly the case with an IT consulting company that provides a variety of services to less experienced clients who choose to take advantage of the opportunity. The client's resources may be inadequate to effectively perform a particular set of tasks, as in the case of an enterprise that doesn't possess the needed people or technology to solve a particular problem or venture into a new area of endeavor. The client, in either of the cases, may choose to focus on core competency. In this instance, a core competency is a set of activities that affect the mission of the client. The use of services may be purely economic, which is usually the basis for most outsourcing.

Service creationism represents a provider–side view of service provisioning.

## Service Evolutionism

On the other hand, a service evolutionist might view the subject of service acquisition in a different manner. With client-side service provisioning, the process of obtaining and deploying services evolves through several identifiable stages of organizational dynamics, based on the three factors presented above, namely value, flexibility, and risk.

Most enterprise processes are comprised of two kinds of activities: core functionality and supporting functionality. In a bank loan department, for example, the lending function is core, and credit checking is supporting. Similarly, in a pension writing department, the synthesis of a pension plan is core, and the back-office computer operations are supplementary. When multiple departments demand the same services, it is a common management

---

[91] An *enterprise* for this discussion is a business organization, a governmental department or agency, an educational unit, or almost any other form of profit-or-non-profit socially constructed organization.

[92] At this point, we are only considering service innovation. Product innovation involves other considerations, although we can easily make the case that all products are actually services.

decision to combine the service operations and in the process, possibly enhance the level of service. "Kick it up a notch" is the usual justification. This is the first stage, referred to here as the *service recognition stage*.

At this point the emphasis changes from operating a service to using a service on the part of the core departments. The core department is avoiding the risks and costs associated with the supplementary function, since service costs are shared. Let us call this the *risk/cost avoidance* stage.

After the need for non-core services is realized and instantiated, there is a universal tendency to reduce costs – because after all, the services are not core to the mission of the organization – or endeavor to make a profit on the service operation. A decision can be taken at this point to spin off the service department as a self-standing internal or external organization, or outsource the total operation to an outside service firm. It would appear that this is either the *spin off stage* or the *outsource stage*, as the case may be.

There are additional considerations, based on infrastructure and management control. Here are some options:

- Outsource the total operation, including infrastructure, people, and management control

- Retain infrastructure and management control and outsource the people and operations

- Retain infrastructure, management control, and operations and outsource the people

- Outsource certain tasks within any of the above options

*Task-oriented outsourcing* is perhaps the end-game in the relationship between enterprise dynamics and service science. It is commonplace in modern business to have professional and technical tasks, such as engineering, software development, and design, outsourced to specialist firms in much the same way that architectural services have existed for many years.

Service evolutionism represents a client–side view of service provisioning.

## SERVICE UNDERPINNINGS

A *service business* is a collection of organizational assets that provide value to clients in the form of services by exploiting inherent capability on two levels: the client level and the provider level. Effective service provisioning permits the client to focus on core competencies.

## Value Creation

The value of a service is determined by a client's expectation of service and the client's perception of the service that is experienced. Expectations are developed by word of mouth, personal needs, and past experience. The service that is delivered is a complex combination of five attributes: reliability, responsiveness, assurance, empathy, and tangibles. *Reliability* refers to the consistency of service. *Responsiveness* reflects the perception that the provider is willing to provide service. *Assurance* is a measure of the competence of the service provider. *Empathy* is a reflection of the personal attention afforded to clients. *Tangibles* refers to the infrastructure as it is related to the service experience. The five attributes of service quality reflect a traditional setting and do not take into account the complications associated with technology driven service provisioning.

To this important list, we are going to add availability, capacity, continuity, and security.

## Availability, Capacity, Continuity, Security, and Risk

*Availability* reflects the degree to which services are available for use by clients under terms and conditions agreed upon in a service-level agreement. Clearly, a service is available only if the client can take advantage of it. Accessibility and expectations are major considerations from the user's perspective. The method of access should be made explicit in the service-level agreement and the user's expectations should be managed by the client.[93]

*Capacity* is the ability of the service and the service provider to support the requisite level of business activity of the client. Demand for service must be available within a specified range and the service provider must be able to supply service provisioning during peak periods in a shared environment.

*Continuity* refers to the ability on the part of the service provider to support capacity during disruptive and catastrophic events. Continued service is not the only consideration. Alternate and backup facilities in the form of services must be in the service landscape.

*Security* refers to controls to assure that client assets will be safe from intrusion, disclosure, and physical safety. Security refers to operational security *and* to the physical safeguard of client assets.

---

[93] The use of the terms *client* and *user* is intentional. Using the principal/agent model, the client is the principal and the user is the agent. We will return to this subject later.

Availability, capacity, continuity, and security collectively determine the client's risk in acquiring services and differentiate between service providers. When comparing the cost and value of services, risk should be factored into the equation.

## Service Assets

Engaging in a business service would appear to be quite straightforward on the surface but is actually a complex arrangement of business units, service units, services that connect the two, and provider types. The abstract term *business units* refers to the provider assets that give value to the client when applied. Similarly, *service assets* refer to the functions that the provider can perform. It follows that a *business service* is a mapping between the provider and the client, in much the same way that we ordinarily conceptualize the physician/patient relationship.

## Service Portfolio

A *service portfolio* is a conceptual collection or list of services. Use of the term is intended to be analogous to a financial portfolio of investment instruments. However, there are major differences depending upon the *raison d'etre* of the portfolio.

A financial portfolio is ordinarily thought to be a collection of assets synthesized so that when the value of one asset goes down, another goes up. This is a bit of a simplification, but it's the idea that counts. The best case is when the value of all of the assets goes up, and the worst case is when the value of the assets goes down. Normal life is somewhere in between. With a service portfolio, there shouldn't be a downside, but some service firms do some things better than others.

With services, the *raison d'etre* of the portfolio depends on whether you are talking to a provider or a client. A provider portfolio might be a simple list of services – something an accounting firm might have as part of their marketing collateral. An IT consulting business, for example, could list items such as strategy formulation, service programming, and operations management.

From the client perspective, however, a service portfolio in indispensable, because it provides a central source of services agreed to in conjunction with the service provider, along with terms, conditions, and service metrics. A related concern is a database of potential suppliers of services.

# OPERATIONS FRAMEWORK

An *operations framework* is a set of service functions established as best practices that assist in providing business value to a client. They should be organized and staffed by internal and external providers involved in IT-based or non-IT-based service operations. The service functions definitely have an IT flavor to them but apply to all provisioning in the services domain. This is an unavoidable situation because most intellectual activity regarding services currently involves IT. The Microsoft Operations Framework lists twenty-one service management functions[94] grouped into four major quadrants:

- *Changing quadrant* – introduces new/change services

- *Operating quadrant* – executes day-to-day operations

- *Supporting quadrant* – resolves incidents and problems

- *Optimizing quadrant* – enhances cost, performance, capacity, and availability services

The functions contained in the quadrants provide the service underpinnings, mentioned above.

This subject was introduced in Chapter 7 as part of a generic services architecture. The preceding list and the service functionality diagram, covered below as Figure 8.1, are repeated here for completeness. Here is how the list of twenty-one service management functions (SMFs) breaks down:

- Changing quadrant
  - o Change management
  - o Configuration management
  - o Release management
- Optimizing quadrant
  - o Availability management
  - o Service–level management
  - o Capacity management
  - o Security management
  - o Infrastructure engineering
  - o Financial management
  - o Workforce management
  - o Service continuity management
- Supporting quadrant
  - o Service-desk management
  - o Incident management
  - o Problem management
- Operating quadrant

---

[94]The Microsoft Operations Framework (MOF) is a contribution to the services field and is an ongoing developmental effort.

    o   Directory-services management
    o   Service monitoring and control
    o   System management
    o   Network management
    o   Security management
    o   Storage management
    o   Job scheduling

All twenty-one SMFs are related, but eight of them are more related than others. Here are the big eight that are more closely coupled than others:

- Changing quadrant
  - o Change management
- Optimizing quadrant
  - o Availability management
  - o Service–level management
  - o Capacity management
- Supporting quadrant
  - o Service-desk management
  - o Incident management
  - o Problem management
- Operating quadrant
  - o Directory-services management

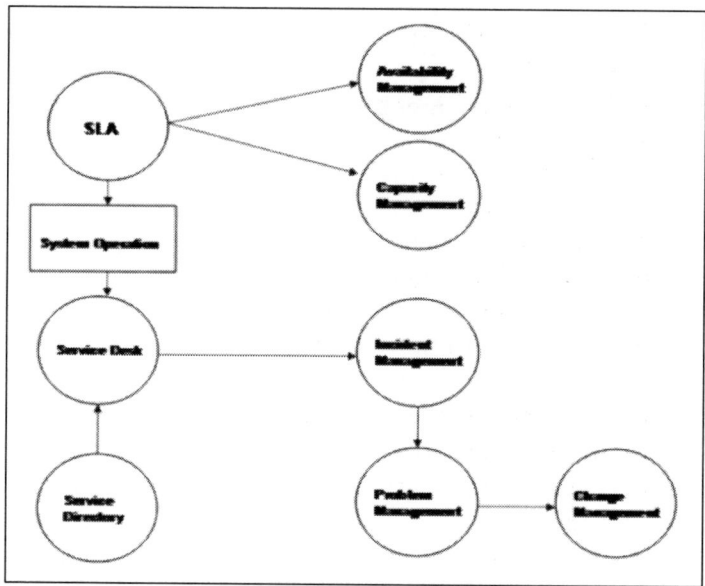

*Figure 8.1 Service Functionality Diagram.*

Collectively, the SMFs agree with the ITIL compendium of best practices. Each of the big-eight is briefly summarized.

## Service-Level Management

A service-level agreement (SLA) is a formal and signed agreement between the service provider organization and the business unit to document expectations and requirements of a service delivered to the business unit from the service provider. The agreement aligns business needs with delivery of services and facilitates delivery of solutions to business requirements at acceptable cost. It involves a definition of requirements, an agreement on specifications, operations management expectations, and a review clause. The tasks include the creation of a service catalog, the development of internal procedures, the ability to monitor and respond to operational conditions, and the ability to perform regular service-level reviews. The service catalog delineates the priority of service-level tasks, the expected effect on employees, a description of users, a listing and description of service assets, and the organization's business partners and suppliers. Service-level monitoring is a key issue. The major service metrics are availability, responsiveness, performance, integrity and accuracy, and security incidents. In order to perform the service-level monitoring, the following steps are required: the identification and criteria for monitoring, establishing thresholds, the definition of alert, the specification of alert management, and essential response definition.

Service-level determination and management is the key element in a service package.

## Availability Management

*Availability management* is the service management function that insures that a given service consistently and effectively delivers the level of support required by the customer. Continuity of service is the key objective. The usual risks to availability relate to technology, business processes, operational procedures, and human error. Countermeasures that have proven to enhance availability are testing of business processes, effective release procedures, and employee training. The areas most affected by availability issues are the implementation of new IT services, critical business functions, supplier behavior, and internal organizational factors, such as policies, procedures, and tools.

## Capacity Management

*Capacity management* is the service management function that optimizes the capability of the service infrastructure and supporting organization to deliver the required level of customer service in the established time domain. Capability of service is the key objective. This SMF is most affected by people, infrastructure, and technology.

## Service-Desk Management

The service desk is a single point of contact for customers and service technicians with the intent of delivering responsive solutions to service needs. The major service desk functions are to handle single incidents and individual service requests. Service desk scheduling has historically been a concern and the current trend is to have self managed teams that utilize service triads or peak period scheduling. A *triad* consists of a three person team, with two people on and one off at any time.

## Incident Management

The objective of incident management is to detect events that disrupt or prevent execution of critical or normal IT services, and to respond to those events with methods of restoring normal services as quickly as possible. An *incident* is any event that is not part of the standard operation of a business process that causes, or may cause, an interruption to, or reduction in, the quality of service. In this context, a *problem* is the root cause of an incident; a *solution* is a method for resolving an incident or problem that resolves the underlying cause; and a *workaround* is a means of restoring a specific incident without resolving the underlying cause.

## Problem Management

The objective of problem management is to investigate and analyze the root causes of incidents and initiate changes to service assets to resolve the underlying problem. The key function of problem management is to reduce the impact of incidents, problems, and errors on the organization by applying methods of root cause and trend analysis.

## Change Management

The objective of change management is to provide a formal process for introducing changes to the service environment with a minimal amount of disruption to normal  service operations while insuring the integrity of critical business functions. Change management preferably goes through several distinct steps: change initiation, change request, change classification, change authorization, release management, and review by a change board.

## Relationship of Key Processes

Incident management is focused on restoring normal service and identifies resolution actions; problem management is focused on the identification and resolution of underlying problems and their root causes; and change management deploys changes developed by incident or problem management.

## Directory-Services Management

The service directory is a database of service assets. Directory services is essentially a database from which users can obtain information on service assets through a secure and organized process that is accessible through appropriate information and communications technology (ICT) facilities. The major directory service functions are to record change events, describe connectivity, track service objects, and identify assets in the service landscape.

# GOVERNANCE

A typical organization has a group of stakeholders who have something to gain if the organization is successful and something to lose if the organization is not successful. The gain could be financial in nature, as in the case of investors, or qualitative in nature, as in the case of non-profit or social organizations. Success or failure is a relative assessment, as is the concept of gain or loss on the part of the stakeholders. The stakeholders, often referred to as the *principles*, give the right to manage the organization to *agents*, ostensibly qualified to do so and are rewarded accordingly, through the application of policies and rules that represent the principle's best interests. The process is generally known as governance, a word derived from the Latin verb "to steer." Agents are often high-level or middle-level managers and administrators, that derive short and long-term monetary gains that are directly related to the organization's success. There are as many forms of governance as there are organizations to control. Even though the words are similar, governance does not imply local, regional, or central government.

## Corporate Governance

The principles of effective corporate governance are well-defined and usually implemented through "boards of directors" and other forms of governing bodies. Governance is usually related to consistent management, cohesive policies, and effective decision rights.[95]

### Information Technology Governance

Information technology (IT) governance is generally regarded a a subset of corporate governance, as it relates to the operational management of IT systems. IT governance deals primarily with the connection between business focus and IT management and often involves the organization's IT application portfolio.[96] IT governance is an important consideration in corporate governance because of the typically large budgets for IT infrastructure.

### Service Governance

*Service governance* is a subset of IT governance to assure the principals that the development and use of services are executed according to best practices. Two factors relate to service governance.

The first factor involves the high-level of outsourcing of IT functionality. The main concern is the loss of control to an external service provider, and also the long-term loss of capability in critical areas of competence.

The second factor is in the evolution to service-oriented architecture for the development of business/enterprise applications. The synthesis of applications from components accessed over the Internet from external service providers constitutes a long-term dependency with which many principals are not comfortable. In this case, the principals may want to use service governance as a means of protecting the long-term interest and possibly the intellectual capital of the parent organization.

## SUMMARY

A *business model* is a representation of a business emphasizing its purpose, strategies, organization and operational practices, and capabilities. It typically covers the following: core capabilities, partner network, value proposition, customer base, distribution methods, cost structure, and revenue base.

A *strategy* has been defined as "A long term plan of action designed to achieve a particular goal," and *governance* as "The set of processes, customs, policies, laws, and institutions affecting the way an endeavor is directed, administered, or controlled."

---

[95] See the Wiki article on governance.
[96] See the Wiki article on IT governance.

A *strategic asset* is a resource that provides the basis for core competencies, economic benefit, and competitive advantage, thereby enabling a service business to provide distinctive service in the marketplace. Because services are labor intensive, investments in people, processes, knowledge, and infrastructure are directly analogous to investments in resources for production and distribution in capital intensive businesses.

The objective of service provisioning – regardless of whether the service involves people processing, possession processing, or information processing – is to provide value to customers through an intrinsic knowledge of customer needs obtained by preparation, analysis, usage patterns, and the application of best practices. Within this perspective, a *service* may be alternately defined as a means of delivering value to customers by facilitating outcomes customers want to achieve without the ownership of specific costs and risks.

The objective of a service business is to assist in making resources available to the client as services, and in the process, creating value for both provider and client. The value of a service is determined by a client's expectation of service and the client's perception of the service that is experienced. Expectations are developed by word of mouth, personal needs, and past experience. The service that is delivered is a complex combination of five attributes: reliability, responsiveness, assurance, empathy, and tangibles.

An *operations framework* is a set of service functions established as best practices that assist in providing business value to a client.

## KEY TERMINOLOGY

The reader should be familiar with the following terms in the context in which they were used in the chapter.

Assurance
Availability
Availability management
Business model
Capacity
Capacity management
Change management
Continuity
Cost advantage
Customer response
Empathy
Governance
Incident
Incident management

IT governance
Mission
Operations framework
Outsource stage
Problem management
Reliability
Responsiveness
Risk/cost-avoidance stage
Security
Service business
Service context
Service differentiation
Service directory
Service governance
Service portfolio
Service-desk management
Service-directory management
Service-level agreement
Service-recognition stage
Spin-off stage
Strategic asset
Strategy
Tangibles
Transaction costs
Workaround

## A FEW GOOD QUESTIONS[97]

1) A _____ _____ is a representation of a business emphasizing its purpose, strategies, organization and operational practices, and capabilities.

2) A _____ has been defined as "A long term plan of action designed to achieve a particular goal," and _____ as "The set of processes, customs, policies, laws, and institutions affecting the way an endeavor is directed, administered, or controlled."

---

[97] Answers: (1) business model; (2) strategy, governance; (3) strategic asset; (4) service context; (5) service business; (6) service portfolio; (7) service-level agreement; (8) information technology; (9) service governance; (10) Service governance.

3)  A _____ _____ is a resource that provides the basis for core competencies, economic benefit, and competitive advantage, thereby enabling a service business to provide distinctive service in the marketplace.

4)  A _____ _____ supports the efficacy of service provisioning.

5)  A _____ _____ is a collection of organizational assets that provide value to clients in the form of services by exploiting inherent capability on two levels: the client level and the provider level.  Effective service provisioning permits the client to focus on core competencies.

6)  A _____ _____ is a conceptual collection or list of services.

7)  A _____ _____ _____ is a formal and signed agreement between the service provider organization and the business unit to document expectations and requirements of a service delivered to the business unit from the service provider.

8)  _____ _____ governance is generally regarded a a subset of corporate governance, as it relates to the operational management of IT systems.

9)  _____ _____ is a subset of IT governance to assure the principals that the development and use of services are executed according to best practices.

10)  An _____ _____ is a set of service functions established as best practices that assist in providing business value to a client.

## SELECTED READING

Carter, S., The *New Language of Business*, Upper Saddle River, NJ: IBM Press, 2007.

Clark, J., *Everything you ever wanted to know about ITIL® in less than one thousand words! Connect Sphere Limited, www.connectsphere.com*, 2007.

Collier, D. and J. Evans, *Operations Management: Goods, Services, and Value Chains*, Mason OH: Thomson Higher Education, 2007.

Fitzsimmons, J. and M. Fitzsimmons, *Service Management: Operations, Strategy, Information Technology* (6th Edition), New York: McGraw-Hill/ Irwin, 2008.

Heizer, J. and B. Render, *Operations Management* (8th Edition), Upper Saddle River, NJ: Pearson Prentice-Hall, 2006.

Hurwitz, J., Bloor, R., Baroudi, C., and M. Kaufman, *Service Oriented Architecture for Dummies*, Hoboken, NJ: Wiley Publishing, Inc., 2007.

Krafzig, D., Banke, K., and D. Slama, *Enterprise SOA: Service-Oriented Architecture Best Practices*, Upper Saddle River, NJ: Prentice Hall, 2005.

itSMF, *An Introductory Overview of ITIL® V3*, itSMF Ltd,, 2007.

ITIL, *Service Strategy*, London: The Stationary Office, 2007.

*Microsoft Operations Framework (MOF)*, TechNet publication, Microsoft Corporation, www.microsoft.com/MOF, 2008.

Wikipedia, *Business Models*, www.wikipedia.com, 2008.

Wikipedia, *Corporate Governance*, www.wikipedia.com, 2008.

Wikipedia, *Governance*, www.wikipedia.com, 2008.

Wikipedia, *Information Technology Governance*, www.wikipedia.com, 2008.

Wikipedia, *Strategy*, www.wikipedia.com, 2008.

Woods, D. and T. Mattern, *Enterprise SOA: Designing IT for Business Innovation*, Sebastopol, CA: O'Reilly Media Inc., 2006.

# Recommended Reading

All of the following books are recommended for a Service Science library. As things are in everyday life, however, some would be more recommended than others based on individual needs and preferences.

Carter, S., The *New Language of Business*, Upper Saddle River, NJ: IBM Press, 2007.

Cerami, E., *Web Services Essentials*, Sebastopol, CA: O'Reilly Media, Inc., 2002.

Collier, D. and J. Evans, *Operations Management: Goods, Services, and Value Chains*, Mason OH: Thomson Higher Education, 2007.

Dykes, L. and E. Tittel, *XML for Dummies* (4th Edition), Hoboken, NJ: Wiley Publishing, Inc. 2005.

Erl, T., *Service-Oriented Architecture: A Field Guide to Integrating XML and Web Services*, Upper Saddle River, NJ: Prentice Hall, 2004.

Erl, T., *SOA: Principles of Service Design*, Upper Saddle River, NJ: Prentice Hall, 2008.

Fitzsimmons, J. and M. Fitzsimmons, *Service Management: Operations, Strategy, Information Technology* (6th Edition), New York: McGraw-Hill/Irwin, 2008.

Friedman, T.L., *The Lexus and the Olive Tree*, New York: Anchor Books, 2000.

Friedman, T.L., *The World is Flat: A Brief History of the Twenty-First Century*, New York: Farrar, Straus and Giraux, 2006.

Gralla, P., *How the Internet Works*, Indianapolis, IN: Que Publishing, 2004.

Hagel, J. and J.S. Brown, *The Only Sustainable Edge*, Boston: Harvard Business School Press, 2007.

Harvard Business Review, *Business Value of IT*, Boston: Harvard Business School Press, 1999.

Heizer, J. and B. Render, *Operations Management* (8th Edition), Upper Saddle River, NJ: Pearson Prentice-Hall, 2006.

Hurwitz, J., Bloor, R., Baroudi, C., and M. Kaufman, *Service Oriented Architecture for Dummies*, Hoboken, NJ: Wiley Publishing, Inc., 2007.

ITIL, *Service Strategy*, London: The Stationary Office, 2007.

Krafzig, D., Banke, K., and D. Slama, *Enterprise SOA: Service-Oriented Architecture Best Practices*, Upper Saddle River, NJ: Prentice Hall, 2005.

Malone, T.W., *The Future of Work*, Boston: Harvard Business School Press, 2004.

Margolis, B. with J. Sharpe, *SOA for the Business Developer: Concepts, BPEL, and SCA*, Lewisville, TX: 2007.

Martin, J. and J.J. Odell, *Object-Oriented Methods: A Foundation* (2nd Edition), Upper Saddle River, NJ: Prentice Hall PTR, 1998.

McGrath, M., *XML in Easy Steps*, New York: Barnes & Noble Books, 2003.

Metters, R., King-Metters, K., Pullman, M., and S Walton, *Successful Service Operations Management* (2e), Boston: Thomson Course Technology, 2006.

Musciano, C. and B. Kennedy, *HTML: The Definitive Guide*, Sebastopol, CA: O'Reilly Media, Inc., 1998.

Potts, S. and M. Kopack, *Web Services in 24 Hours*, Indianapolis: Sams Publishing, 2003.

Richardson, L. and S. Ruby, *RESTful Web Services*, Sebastopol, DA; O'Reilly Media, Inc., 2007.

Ricketts, J.A., *Reaching the Goal: How Managers Improve a Services Business Using Goldratt's Theory of Constraints*, Upper Saddle River, NJ: IBM Press/Pearson plc, 2008.

Smith, J., *Inside Windows Communication Foundation*, Redmond, WA: Microsoft Press, 2007.

Sowa, John F. (2000), *Knowledge Representation: Logical, Philosophical and Computational Foundations*, Brooks Cole Publishing, Pacific Grove Publishing, Inc.

Stair, R.M. and G.W. Reynolds, *Principles of Information Systems: A Managerial Approach*, Boston: Thomson Course Technology, 2008.

Tapscott, D. and A.D. Williams, *Wikinomics: How Mass Collaboration Changes Everything*, New York: Penguin Group, Inc., 2006.

Tidwell, J., *Designing Interfaces*, Sebastopol, CA: O'Reilly Media, Inc., 2006.

Van Slyke, C. and F. Bélanger, *E-Business Technologies: Supporting the Net-Enhanced Organization*, New York: John Wiley and Sons, Inc., 2003.

Watt, A., *Teach Yourself XML in 10 Minutes*, Indianapolis: Sams Publishing, 2003.

Woods, D. and T. Mattern, *Enterprise SOA: Designing IT for Business Innovation*, Sebastopol, CA: O'Reilly Media Inc., 2006.

# *Index*

**A**

A.D. Williams, 75, 195
Abstraction 75, 106, 163, 170
Abstract system 35, 48
Agency model 99
Agreements 2, 37, 95, 160, 177
Airline example 3, 45
Analysis 158, 162, 170
Application service 99
Assurance 93, 154, 180, 188
Asynchronous mode 141
Augmentation 41, 48
Automation 41, 48
Autonomy 163, 164, 170
Availability management 182, 183, 184, 188

**B**

B. Render, 101, 191, 194
Banke, K. 172, 191, 194
Baroudi, C. 101, 172, 191, 194
Bélanger, F. 143, 195
Best practices 99
Bind 141
Blog 73

Blogger 73
Blogging 73
Bloor, R. 101, 172, 191, 194
Body 135, 136, 141
Bot 141
Bottleneck 99
Brokered topology 141
Brown, J.S. 91, 101, 172, 194
Business
  agility 48
  information 55, 72
  model 188
  services 83
Business-to-business 73
Business-to-consumer 73
Business-to-government 73

**C**

Capacity management 182, 183, 185, 188
Carter, S. 172, 190, 193
Caswell, N. 75
Categories 48
Cerami, E. 143, 193
Change management 182, 183, 186, 188

Chat room 73
Cherbakov, L. 90, 100, 172
Choreography 167, 169, 170
Clark, J. 190
Class 16, 30
Client 10, 19, 20, 21, 22, 25, 26, 27,
    28, 38, 57, 91, 93, 94, 99, 112
Closed system 48
Co-production 10
Collaborate 30
Collaboration 41, 48, 59, 73, 75, 195
Collier, D. 190, 193
Component 153, 154, 170, 172
Composability 163, 164, 170
Composite service 48
Concept 16, 30
Conceptual system 49
Constraint management 90
Consumer-to-consumer 73
Continuity 180, 184, 188
Continuous improvement 87, 99
Cost advantage 175, 188
Creativity layer 99
CRM. See Customer Relationship
    Management. 4, 62, 82, 154
Customer relationship management 62
Customer response 175, 188

D

Data 52, 104, 127, 128
Deconstruction 148, 152, 156
Delegation 41, 49
Deliver 64, 73
Description 137, 138, 141, 142
Directory-services management 183
Discoverability 163, 165, 170
Discovery 118, 137, 138, 141, 142
Document element 141
Document Type Declaration 125, 126,
    141
Document Type Definition 125, 128,
    141
Drum, buffer, rope 99
Dykes, L. 143, 193

E

E-services 95
Economic activities 2
Education xv, 93, 190, 193
Electronic
  business 64, 65
  commerce 63
  data interchange 73
  Government 66
  mail 53
  marketplace 65, 66
email. See Electronic Mail. 53, 111,
    140
Empathy 93, 180, 188
Encapsulation 163, 170
Enterprise resource planning 4, 62, 82
Environment (of a system) 49
Equal validity 13, 30
Erl, T. 172, 193
Ernest, M. 172
ERP. See Enterprise Resource Planning.
    4, 62, 82
Evans, J. 190, 193
Extractive 2

F

Find 58, 63, 73
Fitzsimmons, J.A. 31, 100
Fitzsimmons, M.J. 31, 100
Forward-only Server farm 141
Friedman, T.L. 11, 41, 50, 193, 194
Froehle, C.M. 11, 31
Full duplex 141

G

Ganek, A. 100
Gates, B. 51
Globalization 41
Gottschalk, K. 143
Governance 161, 186, 187, 188, 191
Government xv, 66, 67, 73, 104
Government-to-business 73
Government-to-consumer 73

Government-to-government 73
Graham, S. 143
Gralla, P. 75, 194

## H

Hagel, J. 75, 91, 101, 172, 194
Half duplex 141
Handle 73
Header 141
Heizer, J. 101, 191, 194
Heterogeneous 10
Hot link 141
HTML. See Hypertext Markup Language. 117
HTTP. See Hypertext Transfer Protocol. 115, 116, 133, 134, 140, 141, 142, 143
Hurwitz, J. 101, 172, 191, 194
Hyperlink 141
Hypertext markup language 113, 116, 142
Hypertext transfer protocol 115, 116, 140, 142

## I

IBM Almaden Services Research 11, 17, 31, 50
ICT. See Information and Communications Technology. xiii, 41, 42, 43, 44, 45, 49, 51, 69, 73, 74, 77, 78, 97, 100, 104, 106, 122, 165, 166, 169, 174, 186
Implement 87, 156, 170
Incident management 87, 182, 183, 186, 188
Information and Communications Technology 42
Information technology 99, 187
Instant messaging 68
Intangible 10, 27
Interaction service 73
Internet telephone 67, 69, 73
Interoperability 153, 170
Inventoried 10

IT. See Information Technology. 4, 11, 44, 77, 78, 79, 80, 82, 83, 85, 86, 87, 88, 95, 96, 97, 98, 99, 147, 153, 157, 161, 162, 165, 168, 172, 177, 178, 181, 182, 184, 185, 187, 189, 190, 191, 194, 195
ITIL 87, 88, 95, 101, 175, 184, 191, 194
itSMF 79, 101, 191

## K

Kaufman, M. 101, 172, 191, 194
Kennedy, B. 143, 194
King-Metters, K. 101, 194
Kloeckner, K. 100
Kopack, M. 143
Krafzig, D. 172, 191, 194
Kreger, H. 143

## L

Legacy system 170
Loose coupling 158, 170
Lusch, B. 75

## M

M. Kopack 143, 194
Maglio, P. 11
Malone, T.W. 11, 194
Manage 156, 170
Margolis, B. 172, 194
Martin, J. 31, 194
Matlock, T. 37, 50
Mattern, T. 172, 191, 195
McGrath, M. 143, 194
Message 51, 106, 107, 108, 109, 141, 170
Message pattern 141
Messaging 68, 104, 110, 158, 159
Metters, R. 101, 194
Microsoft Corporation 191
Middleware 74
Mission 174, 189
Model 14, 47, 56, 61, 91, 105, 111,

113, 135, 137, 152, 155, 170, 172, 174
Multi-tenant service  99
Multiclient service  74
Multiservice  74
Musciano, C.  143, 194

## N

Newsgroup  72
Nichols, M.  101
Nisavic, J.M.  172
Non-storable  10

## O

Object  xii, 17, 19, 20, 21, 22, 25, 26, 27, 28, 29, 30, 31, 133, 134, 194
Odell, J.  31, 194
Offshoring  43, 44, 49, 50
Ontology  35, 49, 50
On Demand  147, 170
Open system  49
Operand information  74
Operant information  74
Operations framework  189
Orchestration  158, 161, 167, 169, 170
Organization  46, 47, 99, 143, 195
Outsource stage  189
Outsourcing  42, 43, 44, 49, 50
Ownership  7, 42, 43, 46, 48, 50, 160, 176, 188

## P

People  6, 10, 25, 27, 59, 70, 99, 104
People processing  10
Performance layer  99
Podcast  74
Point-to-point  141
Possession processing  xiii, 6, 33, 48, 176, 188
Potts, S.  143, 194
Preproduction phase  170
Problem management  87, 182, 183, 189

Production phase  170
Provider  xii, 10, 17, 18, 19, 20, 21, 22, 24, 25, 26, 27, 28, 29, 57, 99
Provider input  57
Pullman, M.  101, 194
Pull model  74, 99
Purchase  74
Push model  74

## R

Really Simple Syndication  71
Real system  49
Reconstruction  148, 152, 156
Reductionist View  35
Registry  158, 160, 170
Reliability  93, 96, 180, 189
Responsiveness  93, 180, 189
Reusability  163, 164, 170
Reynolds, G.W.  75, 195
Richardson, L.  75, 194
Ricketts, J.A.  101, 195
RSS.  See Really Simple Syndication. 70, 71, 73, 74
Ruby, S.  75, 194

## S

Sampson, S.E.  11, 31
Schema  130, 132, 141
Secondary  2
Security  180, 182, 183, 189
Select  74
Server farm  141
Service
  administration  49
  agility  99
  architecture  x, 145, 156, 167, 169, 170, 171
  archiving  39, 40, 49
  assets  181, 184, 185, 186
  availability  30
  bundle  10
  bus  74, 170
  business  189
  chain  36, 37, 38, 40, 47, 162

componentization 99
Context 175
Contract 163, 164
delivery 30
demand 30
design 86, 99
differentiation 175, 189
directory 99, 189
DNA 25, 28, 30
element 99
factory 49
governance 187, 189
initiation 39, 49
interaction 49
lens 99
life cycle 99
management x, xiii, 86
model 30
nature 30
object xiii, 6, 8, 10, 18, 19, 20, 26,
    33, 37, 47, 48, 79
operation 99
orchestration 99
package 10
platform 49
portal 49
portfolio 189
process 30, 141
provider 94
provisioning 48, 99
quality 92, 93, 98, 99
relationship 49
shop 49
strategy 99
system 49, 141
termination 39, 49
transition 86, 99
universe 30
Service-desk management 182, 183,
    189
Service-directory management 189
Service-level agreement 189
Service-recognition stage 189
Services management 77, 170
Sharpe, J. 172, 194

Simplex 141
Simple Object Access Protocol 133,
    134
Slama, D. 172, 191, 194
Smith, J. 143, 195
Snell, J. 143
SOAP. See Simple Object Access Pro-
    tocol. 133, 134, 135, 136, 141,
    157, 159
SOA reference architecture 170
Social networking 71, 74
Solution lifecycle 170
Sowa, J. F. 50, 195
Space management 49
Spin-off stage 189
Spohrer, J. 75, 104, 143
Stair, R.M. 75, 195
Strategic asset 189
Strategy document 100
Synchronous mode 141
System 34, 49, 54, 75, 183

T

Tabas, L. 75
Tag 141
Tangibles 93, 180, 189
Tapscott, D. 75, 195
Technology vii, xiii, xv, 31, 42, 64, 75,
    78, 94, 100, 101, 103, 105, 155,
    172, 187, 191, 193, 194, 195
Theory of constraints 100
Thick client 74
Thin client 74
Tidwell, J. 75, 195
Time management 49
Tittel, E. 143, 193
Transaction costs 189
Transformational outsourcing 44, 49

U

Uniform Resource Locator 115, 142
URL. See Uniform Resource Locator.
    70, 74, 115, 141, 142

User interface  170
Utility computing  170

V

Value
  creation  41, 42, 61, 92, 98, 177
  net  100
  proposition  10, 152
Van Slyke, C.  143, 195
Vargo, S.  75
Virtual organization structure  74
VoIP  69, 74, 75

W

Walton, S.  101, 194
Warranty  95, 100
Watt, A.  143, 195
webMethods  158, 172
Wikipedia  43, 101, 115, 143, 172,
          174, 191
Williams, A.D.  195
Woods, D.  172, 191, 195
Workaround  185

Z

Zysman, J.  11

Lightning Source UK Ltd.
Milton Keynes UK
UKOW05f0045121013

218948UK00001B/84/P